A GUIDE
TO
HANDLING YOUR OWN DIVORCE OR
DISSOLUTION
THE EASYWAY

Roland Freed

ISBN
978-1-84716-841-2

Series Editor Roger Sproston
Printed by 4edge www.4edge.co.uk

Cover design by Bookworks Derby

CONTENTS

Introduction to this book

INTRODUCTION TO THIS BOOK

In the main, those who have bothered to pick up this book, **(Updated to 2018)**, will be people who want to know more about marriage and divorce, civil partnerships and dissolution or have experienced an initial separation from their partner and are now considering taking the first steps towards finalizing divorce/dissolution. The book will also concern those who wish to know more about Same-Sex marriages and civil unions. When this book was first produced, there was one kind of marriage, a conventional heterosexual marriage. Times have moved on and there are now same sex marriages and civil partnerships. This book covers all three.

It has been fourteen years since the advent of the Civil Partnerships Act and five years since the Same Sex Marriages Act came into force so the question of divorce and dissolution of partnerships is now relevant as quite a few couples have decided to end their marriages/partnerships.

Marriage or civil partnerships can be wonderful institutions and are fine until things go wrong. Everything associated with separation and divorce or dissolution is usually traumatic and hurtful to those involved. A recent study, of 2,000 Britons who have either divorced or ended a long-term relationship, found that 54 per cent had had second thoughts about whether they had made the right decision. Simply realising that they missed or still loved their ex-partner was the main reason for the regret, while others felt lonely, believed that they were to blame or discovered that "the grass wasn't greener."

It also emerged that four in ten couples had tried to give the relationship another try after the break-up, with one in five such couples staying together. The Children and Families Act 2014 now makes it mandatory for divorcing couples to first attend mediation sessions to try to resolve their problems before divorcing, although there are exceptions such as people divorcing because of domestic violence.

Among the other reasons for regret sited by the respondents were feeling a failure, finding out that their ex-partner had met someone else, and realising they were happier in their relationship than being on their own.

This book does not attempt to deal with the more personal aspects of divorce and dissolution, such as the sense of failure and sense of loss. However, what it does do is offer a more practical insight into how the divorce/dissolution process works on a legal level and how you can prepare yourself adequately for these final steps towards ending your marriage/partnership.

As you begin the process of getting divorced, or a dissolution, you may feel that, rather than go rushing immediately to a solicitor, you want to gain a clearer picture of what lies ahead and a background knowledge of the procedures involved. You might even want to do a lot of the work yourself, in order to keep costs down and to exercise more control. Getting divorced, or experiencing a dissolution of a civil partnership will usually involve a lot more than simply obtaining a decree, which announces that your marriage/partnership is over. There will, in most cases, be questions surrounding children, property, money etc. From this book you will gain a practical insight into the law surrounding the divorce/dissolution process and also how these other matters are resolved. A word of caution: it should be remembered that in certain situations it will not be advisable to do it alone without the use of a solicitor. Such cases will be where children and assets are involved and negotiation is needed, or where there are other conflicts.

Initially, in Chapter 1, we deal with traditional marriage then discuss the Marriage (Same Sex Couples) Act 2013. As the marriage Act is relatively new, other than make reference to the fact that the procedures for divorce for same sex couples are contained within the Act we deal mainly with conventional marriages. Civil partnerships are dealt with in Chapter 11.

****

Chapter 1

Marriage and Cohabitation-Civil Partnerships and Same-Sex marriages

The main laws governing marriage in England, The Marriage Act 1949, as amended, and The Marriage Act 1983, states that marriage is the 'voluntary union for life of one man and one woman to the exclusion of all others', although this has now been modified with the introduction of the Marriage (Same Sex Couples) Act 2013 which we discuss at the end of this chapter. We will also discuss Civil Partnerships and dissolution. We begin by discussing conventional heterosexual marriage.

Much has changed in family life over the years and today, marriages break up with alarming frequency and more and more people choose to live together as opposed to marrying.

This section is about the institution of conventional marriage and how it works within the law. We will look at who can get married, the engagement, marriage formalities, effects of marriage, cohabitation and agreements. Reference will be made to the 2013 Act towards the end of the chapter although the main body of the law that applies to conventional marriage also applies to same sex marriages.

It should be noted that there will be no change to the rights and status of EU citizens living in the UK until 2021. A person and there family can apply for 'settled status' to continue living in the UK after June 2021. The scheme will open fully by March 2019.

Marriage

The law states that, in order to marry, a person must:

a) be unmarried

b) be over the age of 18

c) a person can marry over the age of 16 with parental consent

You are also legally a single person if your previous marriage has been annulled. Basically, anyone who wants to marry must be a single person in the eyes of the law. A person must be over 18. A marriage where one of the persons is under 18 is absolutely void, unless parental consent has been gained. If someone marries between the ages of 16-18 the marriage is voidable as opposed to void (see below). Parents, guardians or the courts must consent to a marriage for someone between 16-18 years old.

The Civil Partnerships Act 2004 has introduced civil unions between same sex partners. Through a Civil Partnership, people of the same sex will acquire many of the rights of a conventional married couple. See the end of the chapter for civil partnerships and dissolution.

However, the law of conventional marriage specifies that the marriage must be between partners of opposite sexes. In 2013, the Marriage (Same sex Couples) Act was introduced which now allows same sex couples the same rights to marry as the law covering conventional marriage. There are some differences between the two laws, particularly the right to get married in a church. and this is outlined below. No marriage can take place between close relations, i.e. blood relations, or non-blood relations where the relation is so close that a ban on intermarriage is still imposed. Adopted children are generally treated in law as blood relatives. Brothers in law and sisters in law can marry as can step parent and step child if the step child has not been raised as a child of the family and is over 21 years old.

Marriages must be voluntary

A marriage must be voluntary and not brought about through coercion. This brings about a problem in law when arranged marriages take place, as is the custom in certain ethnic groups. In general the law does not interfere with arranged marriages. However, the courts will get involved if it is felt that there is duress and there is a threat of injury to life or liberty or a child is threatened with expulsion from home or community.

Forced marriage

A forced marriage is where one or both people do not (or in cases of people with learning disabilities, cannot) consent to the marriage and pressure or abuse is used. It is an appalling and indefensible practice and is recognised in the UK as a form of violence against women and men, domestic/child abuse and a serious abuse of human rights.

The pressure put on people to marry against their will can be physical (including threats, actual physical violence and sexual violence) or emotional and psychological (for example, when someone is made to feel like they're bringing shame on their family). Financial abuse (taking your wages or not giving you any money) can also be a factor.

Legislation on Forced Marriage

The Anti-Social Behaviour, Crime and Policing Act 2014 makes it a criminal offence to force someone to marry. This includes:

- Taking someone overseas to force them to marry (whether or not the forced marriage takes place)
- Marrying someone who lacks the mental capacity to consent to the marriage (whether they're pressured to or not)
- Breaching a Forced Marriage Protection Order is also a criminal offence
- The civil remedy of obtaining a Forced Marriage Protection Order through the family courts will continue to exist alongside the new criminal offence, so victims can choose how they wish to be assisted

Forcing someone to marry can result in a sentence of up to 7 years in prison. Disobeying a Forced Marriage Protection Order can result in a sentence of up to 5 years in prison

Forced Marriage Unit

The Forced Marriage Unit (FMU) is a joint Foreign and Commonwealth Office and Home Office unit which was set up in January 2005 to lead on the Government's forced marriage policy, outreach and casework. It operates both inside the UK, where

10

support is provided to any individual, and overseas, where consular assistance is provided to British nationals, including dual nationals.

The FMU operates a public helpline to provide advice and support to victims of forced marriage as well as to professionals dealing with cases. The assistance provided ranges from simple safety advice, through to aiding a victim to prevent their unwanted spouse moving to the UK ('reluctant sponsor' cases), and, in extreme circumstances, to rescues of victims held against their will overseas. See useful addresses and information for further details.

Marriages which can be annulled

Void marriages

Certain marriages are regarded in law as void. This means that, in the eyes of the law the marriage has never taken place at all. Marriages are void where:

1. Your marriage is not legally valid - 'void' marriages
You can annul a marriage if it was not legally valid in the first place, eg:
- you are closely related
- one of you was under 16
- one of you was already married or in a civil partnership
If a marriage was not legally valid, the law says that it never existed. However, you may need legal paperwork to prove this - eg if you want to get married again.

2. Your marriage is defective - 'voidable' marriages

You can annul a marriage if:
- it wasn't consummated - you haven't had sex with the person you married since the wedding (doesn't apply for same sex couples)
- you didn't properly consent to the marriage - eg you were drunk or forced into it
- the other person had a sexually transmitted disease when you got married
- the woman was pregnant by another man when you got married

Marriages annulled for these reasons are known as 'voidable' marriages.

Getting engaged to be married

An engagement is not a precondition of marriage, as it once was. This is often the case, however. A couple will, after engagement, publicly announce their intention to be married. Legal disputes can however arise and couples can dispute ownership of property and gifts. An engagement ring is regarded as an outright gift in the eyes of the law.

If money has been expended on larger items, such as a house, in the anticipation of marriage, and the marriage has fallen through then this will become a legal dispute with each case turning on its own merit and the circumstances of any contract, written or unwritten. Certain insurance companies can offer insurance against weddings falling through or being cancelled. Cover can also be obtained for honeymoons falling through.

If a couples wedding falls through they are legally obliged to return any wedding gifts received to their senders.

Marriage formalities-conventional marriage

For a marriage to be valid, a formal licence and a formal ceremony are necessary. Authority to licence marriages is given to a priest of the Anglican Church and to civil officials (registrars). Every couple, therefore, must obtain permission to marry from an Anglican church or from a civil official. Many couples, because of cost, choose to marry in a registry office.

Religious ceremonies

Religious ceremonies are categorized according to whether they are solemnized by:

- The Anglican Church, including the Church of Wales
- Jews or Quakers (for whom special rules apply under the Marriage Act 1949
- Some other recognized religion.

Church of England-licence to marry

About half of all religious marriage ceremonies take place in the Church of England. There are four ways to effect the necessary preliminaries for an Anglican marriage. Only one may be used. In order to obtain consent to marry in the Church of England you must either:

- publish banns

or obtain one of the following:

- a common ecclesiastical licence
- a 'special licence, also from the ecclesiastical authorities
- a superintendent registrars certificate from the civil authorities.

Publishing banns

The banns, or the names of the couple who intend to marry, have to be read aloud (published) in the church of the parish where the couple are resident. If the couple are resident in different parishes then the banns must be read in each parish church, in one or other of which the ceremony will take place. The priest needs seven days notice in writing from both parties before the banns can be read. The priest has to read them audibly in church on three successive Sundays. If there is no objection from any member of the congregation then, after the third reading the marriage can take place. If any objections are raised, and voiced audibly by a member of the congregation then the banns are void.

Common licence

This dispenses with the banns and is given by the Bishop of the diocese. You must make a sworn affidavit that there is no impediment to the marriage and that any necessary parental consent has been given and that you have resided in the parish for 15 days.

Once granted, the licence to marry has immediate effect and is valid for three months. It will specify the church or chapel in which the marriage is to take place.

Special licence

This is issued by the Archbishop of Canterbury and enables a marriage to take place at any time or place. It also dispenses with the 15-day residence period. To get such a licence, which would for example be applicable if one of the parties was seriously ill, a sworn statement is required.

Superintendent registrars certificate

Although it is the norm for a marriage in the Church of England to take place after banns have been read, or after obtaining a licence from church authorities, an Anglican wedding can take place after a superintendent registrars certificate has been obtained. The parties must give notice to a superintendent registrar in the district in which they have resided for at least seven days before giving notice. They must make a solemn declaration that there are no lawful impediments to their union and that they meet the residential requirements and in the case of persons between 16-18, that they have parental consent. If the parties live in different districts then notice must be given in each district.

The notice is displayed in the superintendent's office for 21 days. At the end of that period, provided there are no objections, the certificate is issued. The marriage can take place in a church within the superintendent's district. The consent of the minister of the church must be obtained.

Divorced person wishing to marry in the Church of England
Where either party is a divorced person, a remarriage cannot be solemnized in the Church of England. However, since 2002, a vicar of a church can make the decision to allow a remarriage in church. This does not apply where the marriage has been annulled.

Other stipulations to a Church of England wedding are laid down in the law, as follows:

- the marriage must be in an unlocked church
- between the hours of 8am and 8pm
- two witnesses must be present

Other denominations and religions
If you belong to a denomination or religion other than the Church of England, you must first obtain permission from the civil authorities to marry. There are four ways of meeting the legal requirements, of which only one needs be used:

- a superintendent registrars certificate
- a superintendent registrars certificate with a licence. This has a residence requirement of 15 days.

16

For those seriously ill or detained, special provisions under the Marriage Act 1983 and the Marriage (Registrar General's Licence) Act 1970 will apply.

Weddings for Jews and Quakers can take place anywhere or at any time under the Marriage Act according to their own practices. The marriage is solemnized by a person designated for the purpose.

Civil ceremonies

The General Register Office will issue a form 357, which provides notes on the legal formalities of marrying. Marriages in a register office require a solemn declaration from both bride and groom according to the civil form:

- that they know of no impediment to their union
- that they can call upon those present as witnesses that they take each other as lawful wedded wife or husband.

The two witnesses present then sign the register.

The superintendent registrar and the registrar must both be present at a civil wedding, which can only take place in a registry office, except in very unusual circumstances where people are ill or otherwise confined.

Witnesses

All marriages, without exception, be they religious or civil, require two witnesses to the ceremony. The witnesses need not know the couple. After a ceremony the witnesses sign the register and a marriage certificate is issued.

Marriages abroad

Generally speaking, a marriage that takes place in another country is recognised as valid in this country. However, all the laws associated with marriage in England and Wales must apply, such as the age restriction and the single person status. It is essential if a person intends to marry abroad that they seek legal advice in order to ascertain the status of the marriage in the UK.

Effects of a marriage

Being married confers a legal status on husband and wife. In general, questions of status, rights and duties concern the following:

Duty to live together

Husband and wife have a duty to live together. If one spouse leaves the other for good then an irretrievable breakdown has occurred

Duty to maintain

Spouses have a duty to maintain one another. This extends to children, obviously, and becomes a particular problem on breakdown of marriage.

Sexual relationship

Husband and wife are expected to have sexual relations. Failure to consummate a marriage, as we have seen, can lead to annulment of a marriage.

Fidelity

Husband and wife are expected to be faithful to one another. Adultery is one of the main grounds for divorce.

Surnames-A wife can take her husbands surname but is not under a legal duty to do so. A wife's right to use the husbands surname will survive death and divorce. A husband can also take a wife's surname although this is unusual. Occasionally, couples will adopt both surnames. If a wife changes her surname to her husbands she can do so informally, simply by using the name. However, change of surname has to be declared to institutions such as banks and a marriage certificate has to be produced.

Joint assets

The matrimonial home as well as family income become assets of a marriage. As we will see, a breakdown of marriage can lead to long and costly battles over assets of a marriage.

Common parenthood-Husband and wife automatically acquire parental responsibility for the children of their marriage. If the couple separate the courts can alter the relationship between parent and child.

Marital confidences

Secrets and other confidences of married life shared between husband and wife are protected by law. This is particularly relevant in this day and age where the tabloids invade the lives of people as never before. Married, and even divorced, persons can obtain injunctions to stop publication of confidential information.

Marriages of convenience

The laws surrounding such marriages have been gradually tightening up. Such marriages are seen as sham devices to get around UK immigration law. In order to issue a person with an entry clearance certificate to enter the UK as an affianced person or spouse, the immigration authorities will want to be sure that:

a) the 'primary' purpose is to get married and that a separation will not take place after marriage and entry
b) that spouses intend to live together as husband and wife
c) if the couple are not already married that the marriage will take place within six months.

It also has to be shown that parties to the marriage will settle in the UK.

Cohabitation

Despite peoples perceptions to the contrary, there is no such thing as 'common law' relationships, i.e. people living together unmarried, as man and wife. As far as the law is concerned they are two legal individuals. There is no duty to cohabit, no duty to maintain. With regard to children, the duty of care usually falls on the mother. However, in the case of unmarried couples, both mother and father can enter into a parental responsibility agreement which should place them in a similar position to married couples in regards to responsibility for children.

If a couple who cohabit and have children, do separate then there is a duty on the father (absent parent) to maintain the child until they reach the age of 17.

Effect on assets

The courts can decide what split will take place in regard to assets of a cohabiting couple. This share is based on concrete facts of the individual's contributions. A live-in partner has no right to occupy the family home under the Matrimonial Homes Act 1973, in the event of breakdown of relationship. However, the law has tightened up in this area. See the chapter on divorce.

Taxation

There are important differences between the tax position of married and cohabiting couples. These are as follows:

- cohabiting couples cannot take advantage of the taxation rules between husband and wife that ensure gifts between husband and wife are free of capital gains tax
- they cannot take advantage of the fact that on the death of a spouse, the other spouse inherits free of inheritance tax

However, as these rules change frequently you should refer to your local tax office for advice. You should also take advice concerning wills and pensions.

Where the law treats cohabitees as husband and wife

There are certain areas where the law will afford the same protection to cohabitees as married people:

- Victims of domestic violence are entitled to protection whether married or not
- With regard to security of tenure, a couple who live together as husband and wife will be entitled to joint security whether married or not
- Certain social security benefits are available for live-in couples. You should seek advice from the local benefits agency
- A duty to maintain the children of a relationship is imposed- irrespective of whether married or not
- Under the Fatal Accidents Act 1976 dependant cohabitees, who have lived together for two years or more may be entitled to damages on his or her death.

Agreements

Cohabitees can enter into agreements to protect property and other assets in the event of splitting up. Married couples also do this.

Contracts between married couples

At common law, a husband 'administered' his wife's property. In effect, a woman no longer owned property after she married. The law moves on thankfully! Today, property that a woman owned before marriage remains her own. If divorce takes place the question to be considered is whether the property has become an asset of the marriage. Each case will turn on its own merit.

In view of the courts wide powers to determine what happens to assets after marriage, few couples enter into agreements (pre-nuptial agreement being the most common). However, the wealthier the person, the wiser it is to enter into such an agreement.

Prenuptial agreements

Prenuptial agreements were not traditionally regarded as binding by the English divorce courts, but there are signs of change. One factor behind this is the increasingly international character of people's lives. So saying this, the main aim behind prenuptial agreements is that at least one of the parties to marriage, be it man or woman, may wish to preserve previously acquired assets from the jurisdiction of the divorce courts. Unfortunately, the situation in almost all cases is that the jurisdiction of the courts cannot be ousted in this way and prenuptial agreements are quite often not worth the paper they are written on.

The agreement will be considered in the light of exactly how long the marriage has lasted and also whether or not there are children involved. English courts traditionally would say that the husband or wife should part with some of the pre-existing wealth if the assets built up over a marriage did not suffice to provide for children's well being.

One relatively recent case which serves to highlight the changes referred to is that of Radmacher v Grantino. Mr Grantino, a French national, married Ms Radmacher, a German national in 1998. The marriage lasted until 2006. They had two children by their marriage. Ms Radmacher belonged to a wealthy industrial family. They came to live in England and sought a divorce in England. By the time of the divorce it was estimated that Ms Radmacher was worth £100m. Much of the wife's wealth had been given to her by her family during her marriage. Prior to the marriage, the wife's family were concerned that none of the wealth should go to her husband so an agreement was drawn up, in a German court. This was drawn up in German, and in the context of German law and Mr Grantino had no real input into the agreement. At the time of the divorce Mr Grantino was claiming £5m for himself and children to ensure that the children were cared for. The court of appeal stated that adults ought to be free to make their own arrangements. They decided that although Ms Radmacher should buy her husband a house he would only have the right to occupy it while the children were dependant. The case then moved onto the Supreme Court who upheld the view of the Appeal Court and that Mr Grantino should be held to the terms of the prenuptial agreement. However, this case involved millions of pounds whereas most don't and the courts will continue to look at prenuptial agreements on their own merits.

Silver pre-nups

These so called 'silver nups' are especially useful for people who have found love a second time round but want to protect assets in the interests of their children. This new breed of pre-nup agreement is helping such couples to avoid the agony of an inheritance dispute. The death of a parent can trigger the dissolution of ties between a child and their surviving step-parent and this can be problematic if a child feels a sense of resentment at money passing to a step-parent. As the number of disputed wills and inheritance claims reaching the High Court soars, many people are turning to 'Silver Nups' to protect their assets when they remarry. This 'Silver Nup' although not legally binding, and not a substitute for a will, can clarify matters. The cost (currently) to create such an agreement is between £350 and £1,000.

There are other alternatives for remarried couples, such as trusts, which can protect assets and it is well worth seeking advice.

Changes to the law

Following Law Commission proposals, first published in 2014, with a draft Bill, it is expected that pre-nups will become enshrined in law. Policy-makers will probably include safe-guards so that neither spouse is left in need in the event of divorce, and will recommend that both parties take independent legal advice. A person won't be able to keep their business intact using a pre-nup if it means leaving a wife of 20 years without proper provision, for example.

Cohabitation agreement

When unmarried couples part, the courts have little powers to determine the split of assets. In relation to cohabitation agreements, there are problems under the law of contract. When parties enter into a contract, both sides have to offer something towards the contract. This is called 'consideration' for the contract. In an agreement to cohabit it would be difficult to define consideration other than on the basis of a sexual relationship. Nevertheless it is wise to have an agreement as a basis, or structure, of the relationship when it concerns assets.

The Marriage (Same Sex Couples) Act 2013 The Marriage (Same Sex Couples) Act 2013 came into force on 17 July 2013 and allows same-sex couples the same right to marry as opposite-sex couples.

Ceremonies can take place in any civil venue and religious organisations will have the opportunity to "opt in" to performing religious same-sex marriages. However, the Church of England and the Church in Wales are specifically prevented by the legislation from conducting same-sex marriages.

The 2013 Act remains separate from the Marriage Act 1949, which allows opposite-sex couples to marry, although the provisions are largely the same and afford married same-sex couples the same legal status as married opposite-sex couples. The term "marriage" and "married couple" is now extended to include same-sex couples.

However, there are some differences between the provisions for annulment and divorce for same-sex marriages in the Marriage (Same Sex Couples) Act and those provided for same-sex couples in the Matrimonial Causes Act 1973.

One of the grounds upon which an opposite-sex marriage may be annulled is for non-consummation due to the incapacity of either party to consummate it or the wilful refusal of the other spouse to consummate it. Although a same-sex marriage may also be annulled, the non-consummation ground does not apply.

In obtaining a divorce, an opposite-sex spouse may rely on the adultery of the other to prove that the marriage has irretrievably broken down. The definition of adultery is *"voluntary sexual intercourse between two persons of the opposite sex, of whom one or both is married but who are not married to each other"*.

The Marriage (Same Sex Couples) Act has amended the Matrimonial Causes Act to add that *"only conduct between the respondent and a person of the opposite sex may constitute adultery for the purposes of this section."* A same-sex spouse would therefore be unable to obtain a divorce based on adultery (although any alleged infidelity with another person of the same sex could be used as evidence of unreasonable behaviour in support of a divorce application).

The new legislation also makes some alterations to the Gender Reassignment Act 2004, as it will now be possible for a transgender person to remain married after changing their gender, provided their spouse agrees. Previously, an application for a Gender Recognition Certificate (to be recognised legally as a person of the opposite sex) had to include a statutory declaration as to whether or not the applicant was married or in a civil partnership, as obtaining the Gender Recognition Certificate (GRC) would have the effect of making the marriage or civil partnership void.

Following the new legislation, a married person applying for a GRC may remain married if their spouse consents. Applications for GRCs will now have to include a statutory declaration stating where the marriage took place together with a statutory declaration from the applicant's spouse to say that they consent to the marriage continuing after the issue of a full GRC. If the spouse does not consent, a statutory declaration will need to be made by the applicant to say that their spouse has not made a statutory declaration consenting to the marriage continuing, and the marriage will be made void.

A same-sex marriage remains distinct from a civil partnership, although couples who have previously entered into a civil partnership will be able to convert it into a marriage by way of an application. The resulting marriage will then be treated as having begun on the date of the civil partnership. Civil partnerships currently remain available only to same-sex couples but the Government has indicated that it will review this in the near future.

Civil partnerships generally and annulment

A Civil partnership is a legal relationship, which can be registered by two people of the same sex. Same-sex couples within a civil partnership can obtain legal recognition for their relationship and can obtain the same benefits generally as married couples.

Civil partnerships came into force on 5th December 2005. The first civil partnerships registered in England and Wales took place on 21st December 2005. Civil partners are treated the same as married couples in many areas, including:

28

- Tax, including inheritance tax
- Employment benefits
- Most state and occupational pension benefits
- Income related benefits, tax credits and child support
- Maintenance for partner and children
- Ability to apply for parental responsibility for a civil partners child
- Inheritance of a tenancy agreement
- Recognition under intestacy rules
- Access to fatal accidents compensation
- Protection from domestic violence
- Recognition for immigration and nationality purposes

Dissolution of a civil partnership

A civil partnership ends only on the death of one of the civil partners, or on the dissolution of the partnership or a nullity order or a presumption of death order by the court. The usual route is for one of the partners to seek a dissolution order to terminate the civil partnership. Other options are available. If one party, for example, did not validly consent as a result of duress, mistake or unsoundness of mind, then a nullity order may be sought from the court. Or if both civil partners do not wish to terminate the partnership one of them may ask the court for a separation order.

The dissolution process

Whoever decides to end the civil partnership may need to seek legal advice. The case will usually be dealt with by a civil partnership proceedings county court, although complex cases will be referred to the high court. There are currently a number of courts able to deal with civil partnership proceedings, as below:

- Birmingham Civil and Family Justice Centre
- Bristol Civil and Family Justice Centre
- Cardiff Civil and Family Justice Centre
- Chester Civil and Family Justice Centre
- Exeter Combined Court Centre
- Leeds Combined Court Centre
- Manchester County Court and Family Court
- Newcastle-upon-Tyne Combined Court Centre

There are a number of leaflets issued by the courts which describe the dissolution process in detail. These are listed under useful information at the back of this book.

To end a civil partnership the applicant (petitioner) must prove to the court that the civil partnership has irretrievably broken down. Proof of an irretrievable breakdown is based on the following:

- Unreasonable behaviour by both other civil partner
- Separation for two years with the consent of the other civil partner
- Separation for five years without the consent of the other civil partner
- If the other civil partner has deserted the applicant for a period of two years or more.

Nullity

In exceptional circumstances one party to a civil partnership may decide to seek a court order (a 'Nullity' order) to annul the civil partnership.

Separation

The grounds on which a separation order may be sought are exactly the same as those for a dissolution order. The end result is different, as a person whose civil partnership has been dissolved is free to marry or form a new partnership whereas a person who has separated remains a civil partner.

The gov.uk website www.gov.uk/end-civil-partnership provides all the advice that is needed to end a civil partnership, including fees.

****

Chapter 2

Divorce or Dissolution-Main Principles of the Law

Divorce law generally

I will deal with the (slight differences) between heterosexual couples and same-sex couples when it comes to ending a marriage or civil partnership at the end of the chapter. Most of the law, and the subsequent financial and child related issues affecting divorce, dissolution of Civil partnerships or Same-sex marriages is similar and applies to both.

Divorce law has developed over the years through legislation made by Parliament and through the build up of "precedents" or through cases decided by the courts. However, in the last thirty years there have been fundamental changes in the way society, and the law, has come to view divorce.

Modern divorce law recognizes that "irretrievable breakdown" of a marriage should be the one and only ground for divorce. This recognition signalled a move away from the idea of "guilty parties" in divorce.

Before the introduction of the notion of irretrievable breakdown it was held that one party had to prove that the other party was guilty of destroying the marriage before divorce could be granted. The law is now much more flexible in its recognition of the breakdown of a marriage.

Since the present law was introduced, making it much easier to obtain divorce, the number of marriage breakdowns in Britain has risen significantly, with one in three couples filing for divorce. This is currently the highest rate in Europe.

There are a lot of problems associated with the law, and the role of those who make divorce law generally. The whole question of divorce law is under scrutiny, particularly the question of whether or not the law should attempt to keep marriages intact or whether it should seek to ease the transition to final separation without presenting unnecessary obstacles. However, although we hear periodic announcements from different politicians on the importance of keeping the family unit intact, and by implication making it harder for people to divorce, the whole climate has changed over the years whereby the law seems to be the facilitator of divorce as opposed to dictating whether or not people can get a divorce.

There has also been a major shift in the law concerning children of divorcing couples. Under The Children Act 1989 (as amended), parents in divorce proceedings are encouraged to take the initiative and take matters into their own hands, making their own decisions concerning the child's future life after divorce. The courts role has been greatly restricted. (See chapter 4)

The Child Support Act 1991 (as amended by the 1995 CSA) has also dramatically changed the role of the courts in divorce proceedings. The Child Maintenance Service, assesses and determines applications for maintenance in accordance with a set formula (see chapter 5) The courts will only now deal with applications for maintenance in certain circumstances.

Law generally – the courts

Before looking at the law surrounding divorce in greater depth, we should look briefly at the structure of the courts and how divorce law is administered.

County courts

Most divorces are handled by a branch of the county court system known as the divorce county courts.

County courts are local courts, usually found within towns and cities throughout England and Wales. These courts do not deal with criminal matters but they attempt to find solutions to virtually every other type of problem facing people in every day life. Such problems might be those that arise between businesses and their customers, between neighbours and between landlord and tenant, to name but a few. Decisions concerning divorce cases, and subsequent orders, were made by Judges and District Judges. However, since 2017, and a reorganisation of the Divorce Courts, a centralisation has meant that 47 Regional Courts were reduced to just 11 divorce centres. Most uncontested decree nisi applications are now considered by legal advisors rather than district judges. This has led, inevitably, in a slowdown and one criticism is that divorces, particularly 'quickie' divorces are taking longer to finalise.

In addition to the judges and legal advisors there is also a large staff of officials who provide the administrative machinery of the courts. Like all administrators, they are the backbone of the operation.

The High Court

Sometimes, rarely, divorce cases need to be referred to the High Court. There are several sections of the high court-the section responsible for divorce and other similar matters is known as the Family Division. However, the majority of divorce cases will be heard in the county courts.

Hearing your divorce case

Hearings related to divorce cases are either in "Open" court or in "Chambers". Proceedings in open court are heard in the court-room itself. They are usually formal and members of the public are allowed to attend. However, most divorces are heard in chambers. These proceedings are private and the general public has no right to attend or listen. Only those people directly concerned with the case are allowed to attend.

Same sex couples-grounds for divorce

For the most part, the grounds for divorce in same sex marriages are the same, but, as stated, a same sex marriage cannot rely on adultery because the definition of adultery is 'engaging in sexual intercourse with a person of the opposite sex. Therefore if a gay couple separated because one of them went off with a member of the same sex, they could not rely on adultery – it would have to be 'unreasonable behaviour'."

Generally

The first question facing couples that wish to divorce is whether or not they qualify at the outset to bring proceedings, i.e. what are the ground rules. If one or other party wishes to file for divorce, the most basic requirement that must be fulfilled is that they should have been married for one-year minimum. They must also be "domiciled" in this country. Both parties must have their permanent homes in England or Wales when the petition is started or both parties should be living in either England or Wales when the petition is started. If this is not the case then both parties must have had their last home in England or Wales when the petition is started or must have been living in England or Wales for at least a year on the day the petition is started. There are a few other stipulations concerning domicile. Leaflet D183 which can be found on the www.justice.gov.uk website explains domicile in depth.

A court can halt proceedings for divorce in England if it would be better for the case to be heard in another country. Usually, the court would try to decide which country is the most appropriate, or with which country the divorcing couple are most closely associated.

Grounds for divorce – the 'five facts'.

As we have seen, there is only one ground for granting a divorce, that is the irretrievable breakdown of marriage. Fundamentally, this means that your marriage has broken down to such a degree that it cannot be retrieved and the only solution is to end it legally. (Matrimonial Causes Act 1973). The person, or spouse, who requests a divorce is known as the "petitioner". the other party is known as the "respondent". Although there is only one ground for divorce, the court has to be satisfied that there is clear evidence of one of the following five facts:

1. that the respondent has committed adultery and the petitioner cannot, or finds it intolerable, to live with the respondent;

2. that the respondent has behaved in such a way that you cannot reasonably be expected to live with him or her (unreasonable behaviour)

3. that the respondent has deserted you for a continuous period of two years immediately before the presentation of your petition for divorce.

4. that parties to a marriage have lived apart for more than two years prior to filing for divorce and that there is no objection or defence to filing for divorce. This is known as the "no fault" ground;

5. that parties to marriage have lived apart continuously five years prior to filing for divorce.

We should now look at each of these "five facts" in more depth.

1. Adultery

Quite simply, adultery is defined as heterosexual sex between one party to a marriage and someone else.

Adultery usually means that a "full" sexual act has been committed so therefore if there has not been penetration then this will not be seen to be adulterous.

For adultery to be proved, an admission by the respondent or evidence of adultery is usually sufficient. The co-respondent need not be named in the divorce petition. If you do mention the name of the co-respondent involved in the adultery, that person is entitled to take part in the divorce proceedings in so far as they affect them. The court will provide the co-respondent with copies of all the relevant divorce papers and he or she will have the opportunity to confirm or deny anything said about him or her in the divorce proceedings. Proving adultery is the first step. You then have to satisfy the courts that you find it intolerable to live with the respondent any further. However, it is not essential to prove that you find it intolerable to live with the respondent because of their adultery. It may be that your marriage has been unhappy for some time and that the adulterous act has proven to be the end. If, after you discover the respondent's adultery, you continue to live together as man and wife for a period of six months or more, you will not be able to rely on adultery as a reason for divorce. As long as the periods of living together after the adultery do not exceed six months in total, the courts will completely disregard them. This gives some room for attempts at reconciliation.

2. Unreasonable behaviour

Although "unreasonable behaviour" is a commonly cited fact for divorce, in practice the court has stringent criteria, which must be met before this is accepted. The law actually says that you must demonstrate that your spouse has behaved in such a way that you cannot reasonably be expected to continue to live with that person.

The court considering your case will look at the particular circumstances surrounding your situation and will then decide whether or not you should continue to tolerate your partner's behaviour within marriage.

The main principle underlying unreasonable behaviour is that it is particular to your own situation and that it cannot be seen as relative to other people's behaviour. You must prove that the behaviour of your partner has gone well beyond the kind of day-to-day irritations that many people suffer and there is real reason to grant a divorce. Examples of such behaviour range from continuous violence and threatening or intimidating behaviour, drunkenness, sexual perversions, neglect, and imposing unreasonable restrictions on another person.

3. Desertion

The fact that you must prove that your spouse has deserted you for a continuous period of two years can present difficulties.

If you are seeking a divorce on the basis of desertion, then it is likely that you will need to employ a solicitor who will need to check rigorously that you comply with the (often complex) requirements upon which a court will insist before granting a divorce. In the main, desertion has arisen because of other associated problems within marriage, and therefore this factor can often be joined with others when applying for a divorce

The simplest form of desertion is when one person walks out on another for no apparent reason. Desertion, however, is not just a physical separation of husband and wife. It implies that the deserting party has rejected all the normal obligations associated with marriage.

Before desertion is proven a court will need to be satisfied of two things:

1. You must demonstrate that you and your spouse have been living separately for a continuous period of two years immediately before you started the divorce proceedings. Although it is usual for separation to start when one person leaves the marital home, it can also happen whilst you are living under the same roof, but living totally separate lives.

The courts are very rigorous indeed when determining that this is the case and will need to be satisfied that your lives are indeed separate and that you can no longer go on carrying out functions jointly. The court will disregard short periods during the separation where you may have attempted to patch up your differences. However, for example, if you attempt to reconcile six months into the initial two year period and this lasts for two months before you separate again, although the courts will not make you start again they will make you wait a further two months before they will hear your divorce. Therefore, the two years becomes two years and two months.

2. That your spouse has decided that your marriage is over-you must also be able to demonstrate that when he or she stopped living with you, your spouse viewed the marriage as ended and intended to separate from you on a permanent basis.

You will not be able to claim desertion if you consented to the separation. The court will take consent to mean that you made it clear from the outset that you consented to separation, through your words or actions.

In addition, you will not be able to claim desertion if your spouse had perfectly good reason to leave, for example he or she may have gone abroad with your full knowledge, to work or may have entered hospital for a long period.

If your spouse leaves because of your own unreasonable behaviour, then you cannot claim desertion. If you are to blame in this case, the courts will not accept desertion.

Finally, because the courts see desertion as essentially separation against your will, then if you come back together again on a permanent basis you can no longer claim desertion.

4. Separation for two years with consent

As with desertion, the particular circumstances in which the law looks upon you as having been separated for two years can include periods of time where you may have been under the same roof together but not functioning as a married couple. There may be short periods during this time where you have lived together, for example, an attempt at reconciliation.

However, as with desertion you will not be able to count these periods towards the two years separation. Therefore, if you have a trial reconciliation period for three months then you will have to wait two years and three months before you can apply for divorce.

The fundamental difference between desertion and separation with consent is that you would not be granted a divorce on the basis of separation if your spouse did not give his or her consent to the divorce.

The court has rigid criteria for proving that your spouse consents to the divorce. Consent is only seen as valid if your spouse has freely given it without pressure. There must also be full understanding on his or her part of what a divorce will mean and how it will affect his or her life.

The court sends a form to divorcing parties soon after initial divorce papers are filed, together with explanatory notes and it is at this point when your spouse will give consent. If your spouse will not consent to divorce and you cannot prove either desertion or adultery then you will be in the position where you will have to wait until five years separation has elapsed before you can seek a divorce. In relation to the above, i.e., divorces granted on the basis of two years separation and consent or five years separation, the courts can exercise special powers to ensure that the financial and personal position of the respondent is protected.

The courts can sometimes delay the process of divorce, or even prevent it, to make sure that there is no undue suffering or exploitation.

5. Five years separation

The final of the "five facts" is the fact of five years separation. If you have been separated for five or more years the courts will grant a divorce whether or not the other party agrees to it, subject to what has been said above. Again, the courts will allow for a period of attempted reconciliation up to six months and the same rules concerning length of time apply as with the other facts. Should you live together for longer than six months, the courts will demand that you start the five-year period again.

Reconciliation

As been shown, in all the provisions of the law relating to each of the five facts which have to be demonstrated in addition to the main ground of "irretrievable breakdown", there are built in provisions for reconciliation. The law is fairly flexible when taking into account attempts at reconciling and sorting out differences.

In effect, these built in provisions allow for a period of up to six months in which both parties can make a concerted attempt at solving their problems. If these attempts are unsuccessful then their legal position vis-a-vis divorce proceedings will not be jeopardized. The reconciliation provisions apply for a period up to six months or separate periods not exceeding six months.

In addition to this, a solicitor, if you have one, will need to certify that he or she has discussed the possibility of reconciliation with you and has ensured that both parties know where to seek advice and guidance if they really wish to attempt reconciliation. The court, if it so wishes, can also adjourn proceedings to give both parties further time to decide whether they genuinely wish to make a further effort to prolong their marriage.

At the end of this book can be found names and addresses of various organizations which can help with the process of reconciliation. The best known of these is RELATE.

Alternative Dispute Resolution-conciliation and mediation services

There is a fundamental difference between reconciliation, and those services which offer help, and Alternative Dispute Resolution.

Conciliation is directed towards making parting easier to handle. The role of the conciliator is to sort out at least some of the difficulties between those who have made a definite and firm decision to obtain a divorce.

The process of conciliation can take place either out of court, or in court. In court, conciliation only arises once the process of litigating for divorce has commenced. It is particularly relevant where the future of children is under discussion.

With in-court conciliation, there is usually what is known as a "pre trial review" of the issues and problems which parties to a divorce are unable to settle themselves. Both the court welfare officer and the district judge are involved in this process.

Out of court conciliation and mediation is intended to assist both parties in reaching an agreement at a stage before they arrive in court, or approach the court. The person involved at this stage is usually always professionally trained, a social worker normally, and who will act as go between. Both parties can also use specially trained legal personnel, lawyers, to help them reach an agreement. This process is like the process of arbitration and is intended to make the formal legal proceedings less hostile and acrimonious. The Ministry of Justice provides details about mediation services local to you.

Couples heading to the divorce courts will have to consider mediation before legally separating. As part of reforms included in the Children and Families Act 2014, anyone seeking a court order to resolve a dispute over children, finances or splitting property must attend a "mediation information and assessment meeting".

The Family Mediation Council will help and assist in this area https://www.familymediationcouncil.org.uk. The Family Mediation Council was established in October 2007 and works for greater public awareness of, and access to, family mediation. They work closely with the Legal Aid Agency (LAA) and the Ministry of Justice (MoJ) on family mediation related projects.

Dissolution of a Civil Partnership

A petition can be filed 12 months after the initial registration of a civil partnership but one of four conditions must be proved:

- The other person has behaved unreasonably;
- The parties have been separated for two years and the other party consents in writing;
- The other party has deserted you for a period of two years;
- You have been separated for five years, consent is then not necessary.

Financial Claims

The court has the power to make a financial order for payment of a lump sum, transfer of property, pension sharing order and maintenance.

On the death of a civil partner the rights of succession are the same as those given to the survivor of a marriage.

Marriage (Same Sex Couples) Act 2013

This act makes provision for same sex couples in England and Wales. It makes marriage between same sex couples lawful and equivalent to a marriage between a man and woman. The term husband will include a man married to another man. The term wife will include a woman married to another woman.

Persons of the same sex will not be able to divorce on adultery or have their marriage annulled for non-consummation.

The grounds for divorce between a same sex couple are the same as those between a man and a woman save a divorce cannot be filed on the basis of adultery. There is one ground – that the marriage has broken down irretrievably and then one or more of four facts needs to be proved:

46

- Unreasonable behaviour of the other person;
- Desertion by the other person for a period of two years or more;Two years separation with the other party's consent in writing;
- Five years separation where no consent is needed.

In a same sex marriage, the parties have the same rights to make an application for financial provision. The court has power to make an order for maintenance, lump sum, transfer of property and pension provision.

In the next chapter, I will be dealing with the actual commencement of divorce/dissolution proceedings following your decision to take action to end your marriage/civil partnership.

****

Chapter 3

Commencing Proceedings

Online divorces

it is possible to obtain a divorce online as opposed to using a solicitor. This may be easier if the divorce is uncomplicated but not so possible if the divorce is filled with acrimony and the separation of assets complicated. One site offering online divorce services is www. divorce-online.co.uk. This company offer three levels of divorce action:

Managed divorce service

The online Managed Divorce Service will enable you to have your divorce dealt with quickly and efficiently, as the firm will deal with the whole divorce process for you, meaning you do not need to deal with the courts. This is designed for uncomplicated cases. This is for a fixed fee, currently £189 (2018).

Managed Divorce with a Financial Consent Order - Fixed Fee

This service involves Divorce-Online handling your entire divorce and the making of a binding financial consent order at court, which will put your financial agreement into legal effect and prevent any future claims.

In order to obtain a consent order, you and your spouse need to have reached an agreement about the division of your finances. You are also advised to obtain one if you have already settled your finances earlier to prevent any possible claims in the future. A pension sharing order is not included as part of this service.

Solicitor divorce with financial consent order

Qualified and experienced family law solicitors will handle your divorce and the making of a financial consent order to put any financial agreement you have reached into legal effect. Any telephone calls, letters and legal advice given by your dedicated solicitor are included in the fixed fee.

All correspondence with the court, your spouse or their solicitor is also included.

With all of the above services there is a main requirement that:

- *You need to have been married at least 12 months.*
- *Your ex needs to be likely to agree to the divorce, but we can still deal with your divorce if you are unsure about this.*
- *You must see England or Wales as your permanent home, or be domiciled in England or Wales if you live abroad.*
- You have a valid *ground for divorce*

Using a solicitor

Although this book is primarily about assisting a person to do their own divorce, it is important to examine the role of the solicitor, in the first instance, in order to get an idea of the advantages. You may feel that using a solicitor would be more advantageous than divorcing online.

The amount of advice you will need from a solicitor will depend entirely on the circumstances of your case and the complexities involved. One of the reasons for reading a book such as this is to broaden your knowledge and put yourself in a stronger position to handle proceedings

Most divorces will have two fairly distinct stages - the first step of obtaining the divorce decree (divorce) and the more complicated problems of sorting out property and financial matters and making arrangements concerning children.

As with most county court procedures now, the procedure for commencing divorce and the subsequent steps up to the issuing of a decree is largely paperwork. Provided that the circumstances of your divorce are straightforward then there is no real need to consult a solicitor at all. In the next chapter, I will be discussing the actual procedure and how to obtain a divorce without a solicitor.

It is up to both parties to ascertain the complexity of the divorce before deciding to go it alone. The questions you should be asking yourselves, preferably during a face- to-face meeting, are whether or not the marriage can be ended with the minimum of problems. If you are childless and there is no property at stake and there will be no financial complications then you should be able to proceed without a solicitor.

If, however, you own property and have children and also have life insurance policies and pension schemes etc, then you will need to try to reach agreement concerning the division of these. This is where divorce gets complicated and may entail you requesting legal advice.

The division of your assets is a matter for you but it has to be reached by agreement. I will be discussing financial matters and children later in the book.

One other aspect of do-it-yourself divorce is that it can be time consuming. Some people cannot spare the valuable time involved and will be happier to leave it to a solicitor.

A solicitor will handle the whole matter for you, when instructed, from obtaining initial information to obtaining a decree. Your main input will be to check over the necessary paperwork at each stage, as required and, in certain cases to deliver documents to the court. However, all of this will be done at the request and direction of the solicitor.

Your future arrangements

Whilst not essential to consult a solicitor, it is wise to at least get a view on future arrangements which you have negotiated. This is particularly important when it comes to future tax arrangements.

If it is necessary to ask a court to determine future arrangements, because of the inability of parties to a divorce to agree or negotiate, then a solicitor may need to take charge of the whole process, although not necessarily as the whole court process is designed to assist people to carry out their own divorce without legal help. Remember, the more a solicitor does for you the more it will cost. You should both bear this in mind when beginning discussions.

Your choice of solicitor

Not all solicitors deal with divorce cases, as this is a specialized area. In addition, not all solicitors operate the "Legal Help Scheme" (see below) which provides for legal aid, although post 2013 this has been drastically reduced for divorce cases.

It is always advisable for parties to a divorce to use separate solicitors over divorce. Solicitors, in the main, would prefer to represent one party and not both as this can present certain conflicts of loyalty and interest, particularly where there are antagonisms. The first task is for you to choose a solicitor. This can be done by either consulting business pages or, perhaps better, requesting a list of recommended solicitors from an advice agency, such as the Citizens Advice Bureau.

You may also feel that you will be eligible for legal help and you should ensure that the firm of solicitors that you choose operate this. Solicitors who do operate under legal help will be marked on the list of firms and solicitor's offices often clearly demonstrate their participation in the scheme by a sign showing two people sitting at a table with the words "legal aid" underneath.

When you have decided on a firm of solicitors, you should then contact them to make an initial appointment to discuss the matter. Your decision to allow a firm to act for you is a commercial one, and you will want in the initial stages to determine the costs and timeframe for your divorce. As there are a number of firms you should at first test the market in order to ensure that you are getting the best deal.

How much will it cost?

Although the costs of solicitors can be quite high, you should be able to keep the overall cost to a reasonable level.

With divorce costs and solicitors charges the first thing to know is that there are normally three possible legal issues involved in a divorce:

1) The divorce itself, obtaining the divorce and, more particularly the decree nisi-which enables both parties to remarry if they wish. The cost of divorce in this narrow sense is quite modest as it involves a distinct process, which can also be achieved oneself.

2) Issues involving the matrimonial property-basically deciding who gets what and whether any maintenance will be paid and so on. The technical phrase for this part of the process is 'ancillary relief'.

3) Issues involving children-access, contact, residence, maintenance etc.

It is the latter two areas that can prove to be quite costly. If dealing with a straightforward divorce then the costs can, more or less, be fixed. Assuming that the divorce is uncontested, there is a court fee, currently £550 (2018) to issue a divorce petition which has to be paid to the court. There is also a court fee of £45 payable to obtain the decree absolute and, normally, there is an affidavit which needs to be sworn during the proceedings which costs approximately £7.50 in most cases. This means that total disbursements payable to the courts are in the region of £602.50. This cost is not cast in stone as there may be extra cost if, for example, the Respondent (person who received the divorce petition) does not reply and it may be necessary to arrange personal service. After the court fees comes the solicitor's charges, which can be significant. This may vary and you will need to obtain quotes.

Legal Help

As of 1st April 2013, legal aid for divorce cases in England and Wales has been withdrawn by the government and you will no longer be able to obtain legal aid funding for your divorce or family law case unless you are a victim of domestic violence. If you are in Scotland there are different rules (see chapter 9).

Check if you can get legal aid

However, you might be able to get some or all of your legal costs paid by the government if: you're using it to pay for mediation; have experienced domestic abuse in the last 5 years; you're at risk of homelessness - for example, if your ex-partner is trying to throw you out of your home

Applying for legal aid

To get legal aid, your legal adviser or family mediator will need a legal aid contract. You can Find a solicitor or mediator with a legal aid contract on GOV.UK.

Your legal adviser or family mediator will check if you can get legal aid and apply for you. If you qualify, the legal aid will be paid directly to them.

Going to court quickly if you or your children are in danger

If you need to go to court quickly to keep you or your children safe from your ex-partner, you can ask your solicitor to apply for 'emergency legal representation'. It pays your solicitor and court fees

if you need a fast decision on money, property or children.

If you get emergency legal representation, you should also ask your solicitor to apply for legal aid for any future costs or court hearings.

If you can't get legal aid

You might be able to get other help to pay for legal advice or court representation, including:

- free or low cost advice from a solicitor or caseworker in a law centre
- up to half an hour free from a solicitor
- free advice (known as 'pro bono' advice) from a solicitor, although this is rare for separation cases
- free advice (known as 'pro bono' advice) from a volunteer barrister - find out more on the Bar Pro Bono Unit website www.barprobono.org.uk

Paying less for a solicitor

You might be able to get free or low cost legal advice from a solicitor or legal adviser in a law centre. Find your local law centre on the Law Centres Network. There might not be a law centre near you that covers family issues, but it's worth checking. If you can't use a law centre, see if any solicitors near you offer half an hour of free advice. The Law Society can help you find a local solicitor. Some solicitors offer more than half an hour of free advice, although this is fairly rare for separation cases. Ask your nearest Citizens Advice if they know of local solicitors who offer free advice. You should research different solicitors before deciding which to choose. Ask them how much they charge and how long they think the process will take. Don't automatically go for the cheapest or the closest. It's important you feel you'll have a good relationship with them.

Paying less for a barrister

If your separation is complicated or needs specialist advice, a solicitor might pass your case onto a barrister. Like a solicitor, a barrister is a type of lawyer so it might be cheaper for you to go straight to a barrister yourself if you think your separation will need specialist advice. You can go directly to a barrister through the public access scheme. www.barcouncil.org.uk/using-a-barrister/public-access

If you need to go to court, you can apply to be represented by a volunteer barrister. You'll need to be referred to one by:

- speaking to your nearest citizens advice bureau

- asking a law centre
- going to a legal advice centre

To get help from a volunteer barrister you need to show you:

- can't afford a barrister - there's no set fee, but they'll normally cost at least £150 an hour
- cant get legal aid

You'll need to apply at least 3 weeks before your next court date.

Help with Mediation

Help with Mediation has its own special rules. It is available only if you are taking part in family mediation or you have successfully reached an agreement with your spouse and need legal advice or support from a solicitor. For example, you may need a solicitor to put your agreement into a legal form so that it can be submitted to the court.

Recovering the cost of divorce from your spouse

It is wise to agree between you beforehand who pays what costs towards the divorce. One of the fundamental principles when handling divorce is to try to sort as much out as possible in order to minimize future complications and also costs, both emotional and financial.

If you cannot decide, or agree, the court will take a view as to who should bear costs. As a general rule, the petitioner will hardly ever be ordered to pay the respondents costs of divorce. A respondent, however, may have to pay a petitioners costs, although not if the petitioner is eligible under the Legal Help Scheme. This depends entirely on the basis for divorce. You can change your solicitor at any point in time if you are unhappy and are paying for the service out of your own pocket. However, you will have to finalize your solicitors bill up to that point. If you feel that you have a complaint then you can complain to the Solicitors Complaints Bureau, set up by the Law Society as part of its regulatory functions. Again, any advice agency will give you details concerning this agency, and how to go about complaining.

The procedure for obtaining a divorce

Whichever way you choose to arrive at your divorce, the underlying procedure is the same: in undefended petitions, both spouses accept that the divorce will go ahead; in defended petitions, one party is filing a defence against the petition.

A special procedure was introduced to deal with undefended divorce petitions, primarily because of the large volume of cases presented to the courts.

At present, there is a set pattern, which you must follow if you wish to obtain a divorce:

a) the petition must be filled in (form D8-see appendix)

b) the petition must enclose a statement of arrangements for the children (if appropriate)

c) three copies of the petition(s) must be sent to the registrar of the divorce county court.

d) there must be sufficient copies for the other parties to the divorce (3)

e) the respondent will then receive his or her copies from the court.

f) other parties involved will receive their copies.

g) the respondent must, on a prescribed form (D10) acknowledge service.

h) the respondent must make clear that he or she has no intention to defend.

i) the documents are examined by a court official (the divorce registrar)

j) the divorce registrar then certifies that the facts of the case are approved.

k) the judge pronounces the decree nisi in open court.

l) the decree is made absolute on application by the petitioner.

Each of the above steps will be discussed briefly below.

The preparation of the divorce petition.

Either you, the online company you use or your solicitor will prepare the divorce petition. The forms used to commence a divorce can all be obtained from the divorce centre local to you. In addition, they can be obtained from the internet (Her Majesty's Courts and Tribunals Service) or from a Citizens Advice Bureau. As discussed there is a fee to commence divorce. The website will provide information concerning fees or this can be obtained from your local divorce centre.

On this form you will record details of your marriage and your children and the grounds on which you are seeking a divorce. You will also list the claims that you are asking the court to consider. This part is particularly important. For example you may wish the court to consider financial matters for you.

Normally, you would include your address on the form but you can make application to the court to leave out your address if this poses any danger to you. It is of the utmost importance that you take care at this stage because you are asking the court to make a very important decision on the basis of information given. You should avoid exaggerating the truth.

A Parenting Plan

It is advisable to put together a Parenting Plan which is a written or online agreement between parents. It helps you record how you will share the care of your child now and in the future. It can easily be changed and is not a legally binding agreement.

Making a Parenting Plan is easier if you both agree on why it is a good idea and what you both want for your child. The first part of the Parenting Plan explains your approach to parenting and your general aims.

Using the Parenting Plan

Your plan can be as simple or as detailed as you like. The simpler it is, the easier it is to stick to. It might include day-to-day arrangements, financial arrangements and decisions about the future. It's a good place to store information like medical records and contact details. You probably won't look at it every day, but it is good to have it available to refer to.

The statement of arrangements

If there are children involved you must fill in another document known simply as "statement of arrangements for children" (form D8A). This sets out the arrangements you intend to make for children once the divorce is granted.

A child, for the purposes of the court is any child who is a child of both parties, an adopted child, or any other child who has been treated by both as part of your family. This does not include children boarded out by local authorities or social services or other voluntary organizations.

Although the courts are not generally concerned with the welfare of adult children (over 16) you will be required to give details of children under 18 who are still receiving instruction at an educational establishment or undergoing other training such as for trade or profession.

The information required for the statement of arrangements will be:

a) where the children will live after divorce

b) who else will be residing there

c) who will look after them

d) where they are to be educated

e) what financial arrangements have been proposed for them

f) what arrangements have been made for the other parent to see them

g) whether they have any illness or disability

i) whether they are under the care or supervision of a person or organization (i.e. social services)

When you have completed this form your spouse should be in agreement. If he or she is not then there will be an opportunity at a later stage to make alternative proposals to the court.

Serving the papers on the respondent and the co-respondent

Once the petition has been received by the courts the court office will then send a copy, plus copy of statement of arrangements to the respondent. This is known as "serving" the documents on the respondent. He or she will also receive two other documents from the court-the "acknowledgement of service" (D10) and the "notice of proceedings".

The notice of proceedings informs the respondent that divorce proceedings have been commenced against him or her and that person must acknowledge service within eight days. There are further instructions concerning seeking legal help or filling in acknowledgement personally.

This document, the acknowledgement of service, is self-explanatory and is designed in question and answer form. It is designed to ensure the court that the respondent has received the papers and is fully aware of impending divorce proceedings against them. The court will not proceed with the case until it has received this information.

If you have commenced proceedings on the ground of adultery then the third party, who is known as the co-respondent, is entitled to be notified of the divorce proceedings.

Non-defence of divorce proceedings

Where the respondent does not wish to defend proceedings, the next steps should be quite straightforward. The court will send either you or your solicitor a copy of the completed acknowledgement of service together with copies of two more forms known as "request for directions for trial" (special procedure) and the "affidavit of evidence" (special procedure) The special procedure indicates that the divorce process will be streamlined. Before, all petitioners seeking a divorce had to go to court and give evidence before a judge. This is no longer necessary. Like many county court procedures the route is now simplified and quicker.

The affidavit of evidence, like all affidavits, confirms that what you have said in your petition is true. You will need to "take an oath" in front of a solicitor which is called "swearing" the affidavit. Any questions concerning the truth later could ultimately, if it is discovered that you have lied, lead to contempt of court.

The "request for directions for trial" is a basic form requesting the court to proceed with your case. Both documents, the affidavit and the request for directions are then returned to court. The case is then examined by an official of the court who will either declare that the facts of the case are proven, or otherwise. If the district judge is happy with the case he or she will issue a certificate that you are entitled to a decree of divorce. Any claims for costs will also be considered at this stage.

When a certificate has been issued, a date will be fixed for decree nisi to be pronounced in open court by judge or district judge. You will be informed of this date but you need not attend court. However, if there is a dispute over costs you will need to attend and the matter will be dealt with by the judge Both the respondent and petitioner are then sent a copy of the decree nisi by the court. However, you have not yet reached the stage of being finally divorced. It is only when your divorce has been made absolute at a later stage that you will be free to remarry if you wish. A decree absolute follows approximately six weeks after decree nisi. If the district judge is not satisfied that you should be granted a divorce, then you will either be asked to produce further evidence or the matter will be sent for trial.

You may be entitled to legal aid if this happens. This is dependent on your income and you should seek advice. If you are refused a divorce, and you have been handling the case yourself then you will most certainly need to go and see a solicitor.

Defence of divorce

If the respondent or co-respondent has returned the papers stating that he or she intends to defend the petition, your next move will be very much dependent on whether an "answer" setting out the defence has been filed. The respondent has 29 days to file a reply.

If a defence has been filed, then the special procedure designed to speed up the process can no longer be used. In this case it is advisable to see a solicitor. There will eventually be a date given for a hearing in court at which both the petitioner and respondent will be expected to attend.

Evidence will be given to the judge who will then have to decide if a divorce should be granted. Legal aid would almost certainly be available and the whole process, depending on the defence can be quite lengthy.

If you are the respondent and you feel that you wish to defend the petition you will almost certainly need to see a solicitor and take advice. In general, undefended straightforward cases, particularly where there are no children involved, can be done on a do-it-yourself basis. Anything more complicated will mean that you will probably need to see a solicitor.

If any other problems arise, such as the respondent either failing or refusing to return acknowledgement of service, proceedings will be delayed whilst a visit by a court official is made. This visit is to ascertain and provide evidence of service. If the respondent cannot be traced, a request can be made to the court for the petition to be heard anyway. Again, this will result in delay.

Ending a civil partnership-procedure
1. File an application

To end a civil partnership, you first need to fill in a dissolution application. (form D8)

You must include your:

- full name and address
- civil partner's full name and address
- civil partnership certificate - the original certificate or a copy from a register office
- Include the names and dates of birth of any children (no matter how old they are).

You must try to find your civil partner's current address if you don't know it. The court will need it to send them a copy of the divorce petition.

Court fee

You will have to pay a £550 court fee to file the dissolution application. You may be able to get help with court fees if you're on benefits or a low income. You can pay by phone with a debit or credit card. The court can call you to take your payment.

Include a letter with your petition to request the call and give them your phone number.

By post with a cheque

Make out the cheque to 'HM Courts and Tribunals Service' and send it with your petition.

Sending the forms

Once you have filled in the forms:

- send 3 copies to the court
- keep copies for yourself
- include your cheque, or your letter asking to pay by phone

Where to send the forms

Send the forms to your nearest court dealing with civil partnership dissolution. The locations of the various courts can be obtained from: https://www.gov.uk/end-civil-partnership/file-application

2. Apply for a conditional order

You can get a conditional order if your partner agrees to end the civil partnership. A conditional order is the first of 2 stages to getting the civil partnership dissolved - the second stage is getting a final order.

If your partner doesn't agree to end the civil partnership, you can still apply for a conditional order. You'll have to go to a hearing at the court to discuss the case, where a judge will decide whether to grant you the conditional order.

You must wait at least 9 days after your civil partner has received their copy of the dissolution application.

Fill in the application form

To apply for a conditional order, fill in the application for a conditional order. If your partner is defending the case, fill in section B of the form, saying you want a 'case management hearing' before the judge. You also need to fill in a statement confirming that what you said in your dissolution application is true.

There are 4 statement forms - use the one that covers the grounds you've given for ending the civil partnership:

- unreasonable behaviour statement
- desertion statement
- 2 years' separation statement
- 5 years' separation statement

The forms will need to show your civil partner:

- has received the dissolution application
- agrees to the dissolution if you're using the fact that you've been living apart for 2 years as your reason
- agrees with any arrangement proposed for children

Attach your civil partner's response to the dissolution application, and send it to the court. Keep your own copy.

3. Apply for a final order

The final order is the legal document that ends your civil partnership. You have to wait 6 weeks after the date of the conditional order to apply for a final order. If your civil partner applied for a conditional order, you have to wait 3 months and 6 weeks after the date of the conditional order. Apply within 12 months of getting the conditional order - otherwise you will have to explain the delay to the court. If you want a legally binding arrangement for dividing money and property you must apply to the court for this before you apply for a final order.

To apply for a final order, fill in the application for a conditional order to be made final. Return the form to the court with the fee. This will usually be the same court that dealt with your conditional order.

Getting the final order

The court will check that there are no reasons why the civil partnership can't be ended. You must provide all details the court asks for within the time limits. If the court is happy with all the information, it will send you and your civil partner a final order. Once you get your final order, your civil partnership has ended and you can enter into another civil partnership if you wish.

You must keep your final order safe - you will need to show it if you enter into another civil partnership or to prove your status.

If your partner lacks mental capacity

You can apply to end your civil partnership if your partner 'lacks mental capacity' and cannot agree to end the civil partnership or take part in the process. Your partner will need someone to make decisions for them during the process. The person who acts on their behalf is called a 'litigation friend'. It can be a family member, close friend or someone else who can represent them.

If your partner doesn't have a litigation friend

If there's no one suitable and willing to be their litigation friend, you can apply to the court to appoint a litigation friend. The Official Solicitor may agree to act as your partner's litigation friend when there's no one else to do this ('litigation friend of last resort').

How to apply

Check there's nobody else suitable or willing to act as your civil partner's litigation friend. Check that there's money available for any costs the Official Solicitor has to pay. Your civil partner may be able to get legal aid. Give the details of your civil partner's doctor or other medical professional to the court so it can ask for a certificate of capacity.

After you apply

If the Official Solicitor agrees to act as litigation friend for your civil partner, you'll be able to end your civil partnership. To contact the Official Solicitor's staff Email or call the private family law team if you have an enquiry:

ospt.dsm@offsol.gsi.gov.uk

Telephone: 020 3681 2754

****

Chapter 4

Children and Divorce

When considering a divorce petition, it is the duty of a court to have regard to all of the circumstances within that petition.

The first, and possibly most important consideration will be the welfare of any children in a family, under the age of eighteen years old.

The Children Act 1989

The underlying aim, or intention, of the Children Act of 1989 (as amended) is that, where there is marital breakdown the law should play as small a role as possible. Parents must continue to care for and to have responsibility for their children until they reach the age of 18.

As far as possible, when divorce proceedings are in process, parents should make their own decisions concerning a child's welfare.

However, should you decide to seek assistance from the courts, the Children Act of 1989 (as amended) provides orders, which can, if necessary, be used to resolve issues relating to children.

Child Arrangements Orders

The Children and families Act 2014 introduced child arrangements orders, replacing residence and contact orders. Under section 8(1) of the Children Act 1989, as amended by the Children and Families

Act 2014, a child arrangements order means an order regulating arrangements relating to any of the following:-

a) With whom a child is to live, spend time or otherwise have contact;

b) When a child is to live, spend time or otherwise have contact with any person.

Child Arrangements Programme (CAP)

The Child Arrangements Programme 2014 applies where a dispute arises between separated parents and/or families about arrangements concerning children. The Programme is designed to try to facilitate and encourage the resolution of disputes outside of the court system and, where not possible, swift resolution of the dispute through the court system. Local practices and initiatives can be operated in addition to and within the framework.

The CAP 2014 endeavours to avoid litigation where possible, with an emphasis on out of court dispute resolution. All prospective applicants, save those who may claim an exemption or whose case is deemed unsuitable by an authorised mediator, must firstly engage in a Mediation Information and Assessment Meeting (MIAM). If pre-proceedings resolution proves impossible, the basic structure of the programme is:

- Application
- Safeguarding checks
- First Hearing Dispute Resolution Hearing

- Case Management directions if agreement not reached, including statements and section 7 reports where appropriate
- Finding of fact hearing, if required
- Dispute Resolution Hearing
- Further case management directions if agreement not reached
- Final hearing.

In certain circumstances prospective applicants are exempt from the MIAM requirement. They include:

- domestic violence
- child protection concerns
- related proceedings being issued in the previous 4 months
- urgency
- disability leading to an inability to facilitate a MIAM
- lack of contact details for respondents
- imprisonment/bail conditions preventing engagement
- non-residency in England and Wales
- that a child would be one of the prospective parties
- unavailability of MIAM facilities.

The CAP 2014 indicates that it is not expected that victims of domestic violence should attempt to mediate or participate in forms of non-court dispute resolution. It is also recognised that drug/alcohol misuse and/or mental illness are likely to prevent couples from making safe use of mediation or similar services.

Alternatively, an authorised family mediator may provide a mediator's exemption indicating that mediation is not suitable as a means of resolving the dispute.

The prospective applicant, or their legal representative, must contact a family mediator to arrange attendance at a MIAM. A prospective respondent is also expected to attend a MIAM, whether a separate MIAM or the same one attended by the prospective applicant. Where at least one party is eligible, the Legal Aid Agency will cover the costs of both parties to attend a MIAM.

Following issue of an application, the judge is obliged to consider, at every stage of court proceedings, whether non-court dispute resolution is appropriate (paragraph 6.1). The court may direct that the proceedings, or a hearing in the proceedings, be adjourned to enable the parties to obtain information and advice about non-court dispute resolution and where they agree to participate in the same (paragraph 6.3).

On issue, and at FHDRA, the court will consider whether the MIAM exemption has been validly claimed, whether the Respondent has attended a MIAM and whether if the exemption has not been validly claimed, the proceedings should be adjourned to enable a MIAM to take place. Some courts will be offering MIAMs and an 'at-court' mediation scheme.

Wishes and feelings of the child

Children and young people should be at the centre of the proceedings and feel that their needs, wishes and feelings have been considered in the court process. Specifically the court should ask whether the child is aware of the proceedings, whether the wishes and feelings of the child are available and/or to be ascertained (if at all), how is the child to be involved in the proceedings (e.g. whether they should meet the judge/lay justices, encouraged to write to the court, have views reported), who will inform the child of the outcome of the case, where appropriate.

Where no final agreement is reached the court will consider what, if any, issues are agreed and what are the key issues that remain to be resolved (both should be recorded on the order).

The court will determine whether a fact-finding hearing should be listed. The court will also consider whether any interim orders can be usefully made, such as indirect/supported/supervised contact.

****

Chapter 5

Financial Support for the Child

Both parents are legally responsible for the financial costs of bringing up their children. If you split up, and you're the parent who doesn't have the main day-to-day care of the children, you may have to pay money to the person looking after the children. This is called child maintenance. Sometimes it's also called child support.

Child maintenance usually takes the form of regular financial payments towards the child's everyday living costs. Depending on your circumstances, you can either arrange this yourselves or use a government scheme. If your situation is complicated, you may need to get a court order.

How do you arrange child maintenance?

You can arrange child maintenance in the following ways:
- a family-based child maintenance arrangement
- a government scheme
- a court order.

Family-based child maintenance arrangements

A family-based arrangement is usually the quickest and easiest way to arrange child maintenance if you can agree. A family-based arrangement is not usually legally binding. So if the agreed payments aren't made, you can't go to court to get the other parent to pay. However, if the arrangement breaks down, you still have the option to use a government scheme for an *enforceable agreement*. This means that the parent who has to pay maintenance can be made to pay it.

If you can't agree on a family-based arrangement

Sometimes it's not possible to make a family-based arrangement. Perhaps because there's been domestic violence or abuse or because you have different ideas about how much money is needed to bring up children. Or maybe your family-based arrangement has broken down. In these cases, you may want to try using a government scheme.

Government schemes

There are three government schemes for arranging child maintenance. Their rules are based on law so they are sometimes known as statutory schemes.

The 2012 Scheme

The Child Maintenance Service (CMS) runs a statutory scheme called **the 2012 Child Maintenance Scheme**. This is open to all new applicants who are unable to make a family-based arrangement. In England, Wales and Scotland, you have to pay a fee to apply to the 2012 Scheme.

The 1993 and 2003 Schemes

The old Child Support Agency (CSA) ran two statutory schemes:

- **the 1993 Scheme** for cases opened before 3 March 2003
- **the 2003 Scheme** for cases opened on or after 3 March 2003.

1993 and 2003 schemes will be replaced by the 2012 scheme over time.

Court orders for maintenance

The CMS deals with all new applications for child maintenance. However, a court can deal with new applications for child maintenance in some situations.

For example:

- you can't apply to the CMS because your ex-partner lives outside the UK
- you have extra expenses which the CMS don't take into account when making a maintenance calculation. For example, this would cover expenses to cover education or the extra costs of a child's disability
- your ex-partner has a very high income and you want more maintenance than would be awarded under the CMS calculation.

You'll need expert advice about what to do if your partner lives outside the UK, and how to apply to court for maintenance. Once a court order is in place, the court can force a parent to pay maintenance if they fail to pay what's been agreed in the order.

Will child maintenance affect your benefits?

Child maintenance is not counted as income for means-tested benefits such as Income Support, income-based Jobseeker's Allowance (JSA) and Housing Benefit. This means if you're getting maintenance you won't get less money in these benefits. Other benefits which aren't means-tested won't be affected either.

If you have to pay maintenance

If you're the parent who has to pay maintenance, and you get certain benefits, you'll have to pay £7 a week out of your benefits if the CMS or CSA make the maintenance arrangement. If you make a family-based arrangement, you and the other parent can agree what you should pay out of your benefits. You won't have to pay any tax on child maintenance payments you receive.

If you have to pay child maintenance

You can't usually get any tax relief on the payments you make in child maintenance. However, if you or the person getting maintenance was born before 6 April 1935, you may be able to claim tax relief in some circumstances.

Legal help to arrange child maintenance

Legal help is not available to cover the costs of going to court just to arrange child maintenance. You might get legal help for some disputes involving children and for family mediation.

The government's Child Maintenance Options Service can provide information about your options. They also provide forms, leaflets and a maintenance calculator to help you get started.

- Child Maintenance Options Service: www.cmoptions.org
- You can get more information about tax relief on maintenance payments on the HMRC website: www.hmrc.gov.uk

****

Chapter 6

General Financial Arrangements and Divorce

Family assets

When a marriage/civil partnership breaks down, everything which has been earned or owned during the marriage is considered part of the assets of that marriage. On divorce these assets can all be redistributed no matter who earned them during the marriage period. As the emphasis is on family assets, property owned by either spouse before the marriage cannot be counted.

However, if one spouse/partner buys a house, or acquires some other asset, before marrying, with a view to living in it or using it together, then this will be counted as an asset.

When a divorce takes place, usually the couple concerned will decide between them what should happen to family assets, the most significant usually being the house, unless there is a large sum of money involved.

If an agreement cannot be reached concerning the division of assets then the couple can ask the court to decide who is to have what. The court has very wide powers to redistribute the family assets. Its task is to try to reach a fair and just division in all the circumstances of each case.

The duty of husband and wife/civil partners to support each other does not end on divorce. In principle, the duty to maintain remains. There have been a number of challenges to this principal however.

In particular, the court must consider whether it would not be desirable to impose a clean break on the couple. This is seen as an alternative to long-term support. It is obligatory for the courts to consider the question of ending one partners financial dependence on the other, once the marriage/CP itself has come to an end. The main difficulties in making a judgement of this kind is that circumstances will vary so much from one couple to another. The main guidelines for the court are:

- How long the couple have been married/in a Civil Partnership
- How old the parties to marriage/CP are
- Whether there are any children involved

If a marriage/cp has been short lived, the parties to it are young and there are no children involved then the courts would almost certainly want to see a clean break.

The one-third rule

In general, if a clean break from marriage/cp is not ordered, then the court calculates on the basis of the "one third" rule. Using this formula the wife gets one third of the combined income-exclusive of maintenance for the children. This is not a rigid rule but the basis for starting calculations in each case.

Factors taken into account by the court when making an order

The court will look at income of each partner, earning capacity, property and other financial resources. This amounts, usually, to the total family resources and is what the court will look at beyond what is said by the parties. Other matters taken into account by a court would be expectations under a will or other family settlement.

The court will also look at financial needs, obligations and responsibilities, both now and in the near future. This covers all out goings such as food, clothing and other essential items. If either spouse has set up home with another partner or intends to remarry, then that second families needs will also be an important factor in the equation. Parties to a marriage/cp are not expected to be in the position that they would have been if the marriage/cp had survived. However, in the case of wealthy or very wealthy households adjustments are sometimes made to compensate for loss of standards. A court will take into account how old parties to a marriage/cp are. A younger person may need less support than an elderly one. If either spouse suffers from a disability or serious illness, this will obviously be a factor in assessing the division of assets.

Pension rights -The 1995 Pensions Act

Under the pensions Act 1995, which covers petitions filed since 1st July 1996, courts must now take pension rights into account. They have the power to redistribute other assets as compensation for loss of pension rights or to order pension trustees or managers to 'earmark' part of the pension to be paid at retirement to the ex-wife/cp, in other words to allocate a share of the husbands/cp's pension to the wife/cp in the future (and any tax free cash he takes at retirement).

The husband/cp can also make a parallel application for his wife's/cp's pension to be earmarked in his favour. The part that is earmarked can either be a percentage of the whole pension or a fixed sum.

Pension sharing

For divorce proceedings started on or after 1st December 2000, (following the introduction of the Welfare Reform and Pensions Act 1999) the courts have a further option: pension sharing (formerly called pension splitting). Unlike earmarking, pension sharing is likely to be a popular option. Under pension sharing, the value of a husbands/cp's pension rights is calculated. Part of that value is then transferred to the wife/cp to fund her/his own pension. The values of the husbands/cp's rights is reduced by the sum transferred.

The question of pension rights following divorce is fraught with problems and was changed significantly by the 1995 Pensions act. Pensions almost always represent a considerable aspect of family investment in the long term. For a couple who divorce late in life, the loss of pension rights can mean a considerable loss of future material comfort.

A woman can also lose the prospect of a widow's pension once she is divorced. There are two considerations for a judge when considering pension rights:

Set off

This permits the division of the matrimonial assets to compensate the wife/cp for any loss of pension rights of the husband/cp that she/he would have had if she/he had remained married to him.

Earmarking

This allows a judge to direct that a part of the pension lump sum that would come into being on retirement, to the wife/cp. Before there can be any transfer there must be a valuation of the pension.

If you're thinking about getting divorced and you're confused about what this might mean for your pension, The Pensions Advisory Service (TPAS) now has a free service to review your options by phone or visit www.thepensionsadvisoryservice.org.uk.

Protection of assets

If there is manoeuvring before the divorce is finalized, for example one spouse attempting to engineer the division of assets to his or her favour, then there are a series of steps which divorcing couples should be aware of which can prevent this happening. The Home is usually the most significant asset at stake and it is essential to ensure that this is not sold or otherwise disposed of without your knowledge.

If your name is on the title deeds of the property then it cannot be sold without your knowledge or consent. However, if you are uncertain of this then it is absolutely essential that you consult a solicitor and ensure that you can register a land charge or notice on the property.

This notice would ensure that any would be purchaser is fully aware of your right to live in the property. If the property was purchased then the person buying would have to let you continue living there.

Protection from the courts generally

If you can satisfy the courts that you have a claim to a share of the family assets or income and that your spouse/cp is about to make off with some of your assets, or already has done so, the court can prevent this taking place.

If you are seriously worried that this will be the case then you should contact your solicitor immediately. It is easier to act before anything takes place than afterwards.

A court can make an injunction to prevent your spouse/cp from disposing of any of the family assets. If he or she does not obey this injunction then imprisonment can follow. The court could also make an order that your spouse/cp pay over money to an independent person for safe keeping, such as a court account or bank account.

If you find out that your spouse/cp has got rid of assets after the event, the process of reclaiming is that much harder. The court has the power to set transactions aside, only provided that they were not made with someone who has paid a proper price and was ignorant of the circumstances.

An example could be shares in a company. If the disposal was to general purchasers, then the ability of the court to get back those stocks is very limited. However, if another party was involved, such as a relative, and the disposal, to that person, was in full knowledge of the circumstances then the courts job is that much easier

Obtaining financial help before divorce is finalised

In the early stages of the divorce/dissolution, you will usually have to rely on your own savings or earnings until a settlement can be reached. Usually, it is the woman who is hardest hit and this section will assume that it is the woman who is seeking help.

Sooner or later, however, you will need more concrete assistance and there are two ways of obtaining this: by applying to the court for an order obliging your husband to maintain you and by applying for welfare benefits.

State and other benefits

There are various benefits available. There is a booklet, at the time of writing, called "Which Benefit"; this can be obtained from your local social security office. This booklet gives up to date information on the type of benefits currently available and your eligibility

There are a number of other leaflets available from other sources. The Child Poverty Action Group, for example, publish several guides and a regular information bulletin about benefits.

If you are in financial difficulty whilst still living with your spouse/cp, you should seek advice about entitlement to benefits from a Citizens Advice Bureau or from your local social security office. There are situations, for example, where you can arrange to have your husband's/cp's income support to be paid to you instead of him/her, if he is refusing to support you and the children properly.

Once divorce proceedings have commenced

The divorce court can order a spouse/cp to make regular cash payments to another to provide for needs until the divorce comes through. This is known as "maintenance pending suit", or maintenance until the divorce is decided (Ancillary Relief).

The court cannot order a spouse/cp to make more substantial payments or divide assets until divorce has been granted. The court can, however, make an order as to who lives in the house until divorce, if the breakdown means that you cannot live under the same roof together.

The court can also take steps to prevent either of you from disposing of any of your property before it has taken the opportunity to consider what should be done with it in the future, if it feels that the disposal will affect future equal and fair distribution.

You can apply for a court order at any stage between the commencement of proceedings and the date on which decree nisi of divorce is made absolute, whether or not you are living apart.

If an order is made, maintenance pending suit, this will tide you over until longer-term plans can be made. Therefore, maintenance pending suit ceases to be payable when your divorce is made absolute.

However, if when your divorce has been finalized an order still has not been made then a maintenance pending suit order can be replaced by an "interim periodical order" which lasts until a final order is made.

When looking at the circumstances of your case in order to be able to make a maintenance pending suit order, the judge will look at the circumstances of both parties and concentrate on achieving a fair balance between what you need and what your spouse/cp can pay. You will both be expected to provide details of your income from all sources and your regular expenses. Assessing your income and expenses may not always be that straightforward. For example, Social Security Benefits may vary depending on whether or not you receive maintenance.

You may have formed a relationship with another person. The fact that you have committed adultery will not normally prevent you receiving maintenance from your spouse/cp. However, if you are living with another person, that person will probably help you to pay for your everyday needs. If this is the case, then maintenance will be reduced.

A good guide to whether or not you are entitled to maintenance pending suit is to draw up a chart which indicates whether or not your income exceeds your outgoings. If you earn more than you spend you are unlikely to get maintenance. If neither of you have commenced divorce proceedings then you will not be able to apply for maintenance. There are, however, other ways in which you can obtain assistance from the courts. The magistrates court can, for example, make various orders to provide maintenance.

The first requirement for an order like this is to demonstrate that you are eligible for such an order.

If you have not yet commenced divorce proceedings

If you have not yet commenced divorce proceedings, you will not be able to apply to the divorce court for maintenance pending suit. However, there are other ways in which you can obtain assistance from the courts.

The magistrates court

In order to obtain help with your financial situation from a magistrate's court, you must be able to show that you are eligible for a magistrate's court order. The following sets out the ways in which you can qualify for an order and the type of order that can be made. If you can prove that:

- Your husband/cp has deserted you
- Your husband/cp has behaved unreasonably
- Your husband/cp has failed to provide reasonable maintenance for you
- Your husband/cp has failed to provide or make reasonable contributions towards the maintenance of a child of the family.

You can then expect to obtain an order for maintenance payable to you at regular intervals and/or a lump sum payment of not more than £1000. If you and your husband/cp have come to a financial arrangement that you would both like the court to put into an order, then the court can grant maintenance for yourself that you have agreed. If you and your husband/cp have been separated by agreement for more than three months and your husband/cp has been making maintenance payments to you and you would like the additional security of an order then a court can grant this order, subject to certain restrictions. Magistrates will decide on a sum to be paid by taking into account your needs and how much your husband/cp can afford to pay.

If you are still living together

If you are living together when you apply to the magistrate's court, you can still obtain an order from the court. However, if you go on living together for a continuous period of more than six months after the order is made, an order for maintenance will cease to be effective. If you are living apart when you get an order, but you subsequently start to live together again your maintenance order will cease if you live together for a continuous period of more than six months.

****

Chapter 7

Protection in Your Home During and Following Divorce

If you are fortunate, you and your spouse/cp may be able to part without animosity when you realize that your marriage/cp is over. However, it is just as likely that you will have to remain under the same roof even though your personal relationships may be tense and strained. In many cases, when your marriage/cp starts to break down, both of you will try to torment the other, to a degree not seen during happier times.

There are many things to consider if relationships start to deteriorate. If you have children the considerations will become more urgent. The main considerations will be: who moves out, who takes care of the children, how will you get them to school and so on.

The courts are able to help considerably with these sorts of problems, and this chapter outlines the various powers of the court to help you until matters are sorted out.

How to get help from the courts

Help is available either from the county court or the magistrates court. Both husband and wife/cp are equally entitled to help from the court, although it is more usual for the wife to seek help. In some cases, it may be more appropriate for each of you to ask the court to intervene in some way.

It is not necessary for either of you to have started divorce proceedings before you apply, nor essential that you are still living together. Neither does it matter who owns the house or whose name it is in.

Help from the magistrate's court

The magistrate's court can make orders protecting you or a child of the family from your spouse/cp. These are called "personal protection orders". Before you can get a personal protection order, you will have to satisfy the court of the following:

- that your spouse/cp has used violence or threatened to use violence against you and a child of the family and;
- that you need to be protected from him/her by an order of the court;

If you can satisfy these conditions, the court can make an order preventing your spouse/cp from using or threatening violence against you and/or your family.

The magistrate's court can also make an order excluding your spouse/cp from your home. This is called an "exclusion order". The magistrates will only make an exclusion order if your case is serious.

If your spouse/cp has already been violent towards you or a child of the family, you must be able to show that you or the child are in danger of being physically injured by him/her, or would be if he were to be allowed into the home.

If your spouse/cp has not actually been violent towards you or a child yet, you will have to demonstrate;

- that you or a child are in danger of being physically injured by him/her and;
- that he/she has threatened you or a child with violence and by doing so he was breaking an existing personal protection order already in force, or alternatively, that he/she has threatened you or a child with violence, and he/she has already demonstrated that they are capable of violent behaviour by using violence on someone else.

If necessary, when it makes an exclusion order the court can also order your spouse/cp to allow you to return to live in the home. This might be appropriate, for example, if there was a serious risk that your spouse would move out as directed but at the same time change all the locks so that you could not get back into the property.

Help from the county court

There is a wide range of orders available from the county court. They fall into two categories; "non-molestation orders" and "exclusion orders". The technical name for an order of either type is an injunction. The 1996 Family Law Act has strengthened these provisions.

Non-molestation injunctions

The court can make an order prohibiting your spouse/cp from molesting you or your children. This order is roughly the equivalent of the magistrate's personal protection order, although the county court is able to protect you not only from violence but from a wider range of behaviour on the part of your spouse/cp.

Exclusion injunctions

The court can exclude your spouse/cp from the family home and even from the immediate vicinity of the house and can also order him/her to permit you to return to live there if he/she has turned you out, or is preventing you from entering.

The court will not make this sort of order lightly. It must be fair, just and reasonable to do so. There are many factors to be taken into account including the behaviour of each of you, and both your personal circumstances. For instance, what, if any, alternative accommodation you would each be able to find if you had to leave, whether either of you will suffer injury to your physical or mental health if you have to go on living in the same house, and so on.

If you have children, the court will concentrate particularly on how the situation is affecting them. It will want to know how much it is distressing the children to see the relationship between you and your spouse/cp deteriorate, what effect it would have on them if your spouse/cp was ordered to leave and how they would be affected if he/she was to stay; whether they are, in fact, being directly involved in the breakdown of your marriage/cp, perhaps because your spouse has threatened violence towards them.

When the court has all the information necessary, it is likely to approach its decision on the house in two parts. It will first decide whether the situation has got so bad that you can no longer go on living together as a family in the same house. If it considers that this is so, it has then got to decide how things can be arranged so that you and your spouse/cp do not come into contact any more than is necessary.

If your house is small then the court may have no choice but to order you both out. If you have more room, it may be possible for the court to divide up the house and allocate part to each of you so you both have separate space.

If you have children, the courts decision will usually be determined by what is going to happen to the children. The parent who is going to look after them will normally be allowed to stay in the house while the other will have to move out. If there are no children, the court will decide what should be done by looking at the way you have both behaved and assessing which of you would be better able to fend for yourself if turned out of your home. If one of you has obviously behaved far more unreasonably than the other, that person can usually expect to be the one asked or ordered to leave.

If there is a serious possibility of your spouse/cp making a nuisance of him/her self in the vicinity of the house at any time after he/she has been ordered to leave, the court can be asked to make a further order prohibiting him/her from coming within a specified distance of the house. As with a non-molestation injunction, it is worth remembering that an exclusion injunction will not be granted unless there is real reason. If you are asking the court for such an order you will have to attend court to give evidence about your circumstances, and you may also have to swear an affidavit setting out in writing why you need the courts help. Your spouse will also usually have the opportunity to give evidence at the court hearing.

It is up to the court to decide how long its order should last. It will generally specify the duration of the order when it makes it

Personal protection orders and non-molestation injunctions will generally last until you are divorced although the court can grant an injunction for a shorter or longer period. Exclusion orders and injunctions do not generally last for as long as the above orders. They are not intended to resolve the question of your accommodation for good but to tide you over until you can make alternative arrangements or take divorce/dissolution proceedings so that the court has an opportunity to deal with long-term arrangements for your family property.

If either party wants the terms of the order or the injunction discharged completely you are free to ask the court to make a further order.

Living together whilst the court order is in force

Non-molestation injunctions and personal protection orders do not necessarily mean that you will be living separately, they simply regulate your conduct towards each other. However, an exclusion order will mean that you will be living apart. If you both want to give things another try and start living together again, you are perfectly free to do so without referring to the court.

If this is the case and your spouse/cp feels that he/she would rather not have the exclusion order hanging over them then he/she can apply to the court to have it discharged.

Seeing the children when the court order is in force

Provided that your spouse/cp has not been specifically prevented by the court from seeing the children he/she will normally be entitled to do so even though a personal protection order or non molestation order is in force or he/she has been excluded from the home.

However, you may have to be prepared to alter your arrangements over contact to make sure that they do not involve your spouse/cp breaking the court order.

How quickly can you get a court order?

In a normal case, the court will not deal with your application until your spouse/cp has been notified of it and given a chance to attend at court to put his/her side of the story.

If you urgently need help because you or a child of the family are in imminent danger of being seriously injured by your spouse/cp, the court can immediately act without your spouse/cp even knowing that you have made an application. If the court makes an emergency application in this way, the order is described as an "ex parte" order (in the county court). In the magistrate's court it is described as an "expedited order".

As a general rule, you will not be able to obtain an exclusion order by this emergency procedure-the only protection you will be given will be in the form of a non-molestation order or personal protection order.

In a really urgent case, it is possible to apply to a judge of the county court for an injunction, even outside court hours, but this is not possible in the magistrate's court, which can only deal with applications during court time.

An emergency order will only be temporary. In the county court, it will last until the earliest possible date when the whole case can be considered in full with an opportunity for your spouse to have his say. An order of the magistrate's court made in an emergency can only last for a maximum of 28 days, even if there has not been an opportunity for a full investigation of the case before then. However, you can apply for it to be renewed at the end of the 28-day period. The time actually taken to obtain an order, either in an emergency or in the normal way, will depend on all the circumstances-not only what your case involves but also how busy the court is.

Undertakings to the court

If you have made an application to the county court, and your spouse/cp is willing to promise that he/she will not molest you or will move out of the house within a certain length of time he/she may give the court an undertaking that this will be the case. Breach of this undertaking can mean heavy penalties.

Enabling a court order

If the courts order is not obeyed, then the next step in the process depends very much whether or not there is a "power of arrest" within the court order. This is a special order entitling the police to arrest your spouse/cp straight away if he/she breaks the court order. If the court makes an order prohibiting your spouse/cp from using violence towards you or a child of the family or excluding him/her from the home, and it is satisfied that he/she has already injured you or a child of the family, it can grant a power of arrest. If a power of arrest is granted with your order, and your spouse/cp breaks the courts order by using violence towards you or the child or by entering the house or the surrounding area after he/she has been excluded, you should contact your local police station. The police will normally arrest your spouse/cp at once. If he/she is arrested, he/she will be kept in custody and brought before the court within 24 hours. The court will have to decide what should be done about your spouse's/cp's conduct. It can send him/her immediately to prison for whatever period it thinks appropriate. However, this is unlikely to happen if it is the first time he/she has broken the injunction or order, as imprisonment is usually reserved as something of a last resort for people who have persistently disobeyed the courts orders. Alternatively, the court can fine your spouse/cp.

In addition to the above, there are other measures that the court can take. For example, the court may decide to modify the original order in the light of what has happened. If you are not granted a power of arrest, it is up to you, with your solicitor's help, to take steps to bring your spouse/cp back to court if he/she breaks the order so that the court can decide what is to be done. The proceedings described so far in this chapter are "civil proceedings", in other words, they do not involve a criminal prosecution. However, if your spouse/cp assaults you or damages your property, he/she will have committed a criminal offence.

The police would be reluctant to take action though without a power of arrest. If you are dissatisfied that the police are not prosecuting your spouse/cp, you may be able to bring a criminal prosecution against him/her yourself. You should, however, think carefully before going down this road because of the stress and the expense.

****

Chapter 8

Other Considerations

Remarriage

You are only free to remarry or enter into another civil partnership when your divorce/dissolution is made final by decree absolute or final order. Before you are allowed to marry in any church or registry office, you will need to produce a copy of the decree absolute or final order.

When you remarry, your entitlement to regular payments from your spouse/cp will cease. This is not the case for children, who will continue to be entitled.

Orders that have already been made in relation to your property and capital will not, however, be affected by your remarriage/new civil partnership.

If the spouse/cp who has an obligation to make frequent payments remarries, this will not alter his/her liability to continue to make these payments. Liability can only be reduced or extinguished if it can be demonstrated that his or her circumstances have changed as a result of re-marriage, which would affect ability to pay.

Once you have remarried/entered into another civil partnership, you are no longer entitled to begin a claim for property adjustment orders or for a lump sum payment. This is not the case if you have started the claim before you remarry, you will be allowed to continue with it. You should ensure that all necessary claims to property and other assets are in place before you remarry/enter into another civil partnership. Your solicitor will help you with this if necessary. Your rights in relation to children will usually be totally unaffected by remarriage/new CP. However, in the unlikely event of your remarrying someone totally unsuitable to be in contact with your children, you could find that your ex-spouse/cp will apply for an order depriving you of contact with them.

Tax tips when separating

There are tax implications to consider when deciding to separate and divorce/seek a dissolution. Tax can be an issue and cause headaches further down the line. There are certain rules that divorcing couples should follow to minimise the potential tax bills.

Separate with care

One vital piece of advice here is never walk out on your spouse/cp on April the 5th. Time the divorce/separation date after the start of the new tax year on 6th April. This may sound mechanical but it can save you thousands of pounds. This is because a number of tax breaks available when married or in a civil partnership disappear when divorced/separated. The most significant being the ability to transfer assets to your spouse without any Capital Gains Tax (CGT) owing. This special exemption disappears at midnight on the 5th of April after you permanently separated, not upon divorce.

In addition, if couples want to swap assets, such as shares, rental properties, second homes, paintings, jewellery etc then this should be done before the 5th of April as there may be adverse tax implications.

If it is too late to take advantage of this exemption, then you may still be able to transfer your share of the family home to your ex spouse/cp, or vice versa, using principle private residence tax relief (PPR). Under this perk, the last 18 months of ownership are always exempt from CGT, provided that at some point the property has been your main residence. As part of the divorce settlement, you may be able to extend the period to avoid an immediate sale. There are certain provisos however on which you will certainly need advice if you are going down this route.

Make sure you are very clear on the tax implications of divorce as this will save you a lot of trouble in the future.

Income tax

People generally are affected by three forms of tax during their lives-income tax, inheritance tax and capital gains tax.

Inheritance tax is complicated. This is the tax payable on your assets when you pass away and on any money or property you have transferred within seven years of your death. You will not normally need to involve yourself with inheritance tax at the time of divorce/dissolution.

Capital gains tax is far more relevant to divorcing couples. This form of taxation is payable on capital gains that are made when you are disposing of property during your lifetime. Her Majesty's Revenue and Customs treat property given away as "disposed of". This therefore attracts a capital gain, or is treated as a capital gain.

Although you will be liable for capital gains tax when you dispose of property, you would not do so if you gave away money. This is exempt. There are also other exemptions from capital gains tax, for example you are permitted to make gains each year on property values. You should check with HMRC for the latest figures.

The tax position when living together as a couple

Income tax. Everyone is entitled to a tax-free element within their income each year, known as the personal allowance. This amount will vary according to your circumstances, i.e. whether you are married or single.

After 6th of April 1990, the system of joining husband and wife's income together for tax purposes ended and a new system introduced. Now husband and wife/civil partner are taxed separately on their earned and investment income. Each has a single persons allowance.

In addition to this, there is still a married couples allowance which is normally set against a husbands income but can also be set against a woman's earnings. However, both of the partners can claim half of the allowance which will be split equally between them.

Capital gains tax is also no longer combined and a husband and wife/civil partner will also be taxed independently on his or her capital gains and will be entitled to a tax free allowance to set against them.

While you live together as husband and wife/civil partner you can dispose of property to each other without incurring a capital gains tax. However, if the property is disposed of later to someone else then a capital gains tax is payable.

The tax position when living apart

As we have seen, separation will affect your tax position. For tax purposes, you are living apart if you are separated under a court order or a deed of Separation or you are separated in such a way, or circumstance, that your Separation is likely to be permanent.

HMRC imposes special rules during the year that you separate. Each person will have a single persons allowance and there will be a married couple's allowance, which will be split, as it was when you separated. If you have any of the children living with you who are under 16, or over 16 and still undergoing further education at school, university or other college, you may be able to claim an additional personal allowance for the remainder of the year of separation but not if you are already receiving the full married couples allowance. After the end of the tax year in which you separate:

- you both continue to be taxed as individuals on your earned and unearned income. You will each be responsible to HMRC in respect of your own tax.
- normally, you will both only get a single persons allowance

Either one or both of you may be able to claim the additional personal allowance if you are looking after one or more of the children. Separated spouses/civil partners are treated as single people for the purposes of capital gains tax. During the first year, or the tax year within which you separate you can make tax free disposals to your spouse. After that ends, so does this right.

After divorce/dissolution

Most of the tax changes experienced by yourself will happen when you cease to live together. The act of divorce/dissolution only finalizes these changes.

Maintenance payments and income tax

In 1988, the treatment of maintenance payments, and the tax position was simplified. Although certain of the older orders and maintenance agreements remain under older rules, all other orders are subject to the new rules as set out below.

The payer

If the court orders that you make maintenance payments to a spouse/cp, or ex-spouse/cp either for his or her own benefit, or a child's benefit, or you enter into a legally binding agreement to do so then you should get tax relief on the payments.

You will get this tax relief through your PAYE code or tax assessment.

Relief for your maintenance payments will continue if you remarry/enter into a new civil partnership but will cease if your spouse/cp does. For the recipient the maintenance you receive will be tax-free. This also applies to your children.

Sharing out property and capital gains tax

Until you separate, and in the year of separation, you can make whatever re-allocation of assets between you that you like without any immediate liability to Capital Gains Tax.

After you separate, and following the end of that particular tax year, gains that you make when transferring property to your spouse/cp could be liable to Capital Gains Tax depending on the type of property involved. As stated previously, you can share out savings but if you have to sell an item to pay of your spouse then you may be liable to pay tax.

When you dispose of your house to your spouse/cp, or previous spouse/cp, it is not always possible to escape entirely from Capital Gains Tax. This is because any gain which is made when disposing of a property that was your main home is exempt from Capital Gains Tax provided that you have been absent from it for more than three years and that no other house has replaced it as your residence, or main residence.

Even if you have moved out more than three years ago, you may still escape Capital Gains Tax if you transfer an interest in the house to your spouse/cp as part of a financial settlement on divorce or separation, provided your spouse/cp has continued to occupy the house as her only main home.

Enforcing court orders and agreements

Problems usually arise over payment of maintenance, in that they are sporadic or stop altogether. However, problems do also arise over arrangements for property. Courts can resolve problems such as these.

Maintenance problems

If you have come to a formal agreement with your spouse/cp concerning payment of maintenance and your spouse/cp fails to pay, the courts can order him or her to pay as agreed. This is the same if the order has been made by the court and is broken. The method of enforcement will depend on which court made the order.

Enforcement in the magistrate's court

If the court order has been registered in the magistrate's court, because problems of future payments were foreseen, then it is the responsibility of the magistrate's court to chase up non-payment.

Magistrate's courts can take several different views about non-payment. They can, for example, decide that your spouse/cp should be excused from some or all arrears. This does not excuse your spouse/cp from future liability. The Magistrates court can also make arrangements for your spouse/cp to pay off the arrears in instalments along with the current maintenance due.

An attachment of earnings order can also be made. It is addressed to the employer, if one exists and directs the paying of frequent sums of money from the spouse's/cp's earnings. The court can also order that your spouse/cp be sent to prison for non-payment of maintenance. This is usually a last resort but is a frequent occurrence, as Her Majesties Prisons will testify. If you receive regular payments of income support, because of the low level of maintenance paid by your spouse/cp, you may want to make over your maintenance order to the Department of Work and Pensions. This means that the magistrate's court will pay over sums to the DWP instead of you. You will then be entitled to draw full income support, irrespective of what is paid to you by your spouse/CP.

If your order has not been registered in the magistrate's court it will be up to you to take your spouse/cp back before the magistrate's court to get an order to pay. You should keep a clear and accurate record of payments made to you. If your spouse/cp goes abroad, then the act of collecting unpaid maintenance becomes that much harder and you will need help from a solicitor in deciding a way forward.

Variations of agreements in the future

The courts have powers to vary orders at a later date if circumstances change.

Maintenance orders

You are more likely to require a change in the divorce courts maintenance order than in any other court order. Although the court will vary orders, you have to put forward a good case for the change. If you were awarded or ordered to pay a lump sum in one instalment, the court will not be able to alter this order on a subsequent occasion. If the lump sum is paid in more than one instalment then this can be altered. If the court made an order in relation to your property on your divorce neither of you can ask for this order to be varied at a later date. However, if the court granted you "liberty to apply" or ordered a sale on some of your property when it made the order, you can seek further assistance in putting the order into practice.

Changing your will

Like almost everyone, during marriage all of your property and assets (estate) would normally be made out to your partner. However, on breakdown of marriage it is usual for your will, if you have one, to be substantially altered.

If you die without making a will, this is known as dying intestate. If you die intestate before decree absolute of divorce/final order is granted, as a general rule all your personal belongings will pass to your spouse/cp, together with a substantial proportion of your money and your interests in land.

If you die intestate after the divorce is finalized, your spouse/cp will have no automatic right to any of your estate. Your children would probably inherit the estate. However, provided your spouse/cp has not remarried, he or she can make an application to the court for a share of the estate on the grounds that provision for his or her maintenance should have been made after your death.

If you have a will

If you die after decree absolute/final order has been granted leaving a will made before you were divorced, then unless it is clear that your intention is for the former spouses/cp's position to be unaffected by the divorce, anything left to him or her will automatically become ineffective, as will any appointment of him as your executor.

If you die before Decree Absolute/final order your spouse/cp will still be able to benefit from the will. It is advisable to produce a fresh will which takes into account your new circumstances following divorce and possible remarriage. Surprisingly, this is one area which is very neglected and which causes a lot of pain and anxiety following divorce and the death of one or other partner.

****

Chapter 9

Marriage and Divorce/Dissolution in Scotland

The Marriage and Civil Partnership (Scotland) Act 2014 received Royal Assent on 12 March 2014. The first ceremonies took place on 31 December 2014.

Who can be married in Scotland?

Any two persons, regardless of sex or where they live, may marry in Scotland provided that:

- Both persons are at least 16 years of age on the day of their marriage.
- They are not related to one another in a way which would prevent their marrying
- They are unmarried and not in a civil partnership
- They are capable of understanding the nature of a marriage ceremony and of consenting to marrying.
- In the case of an opposite sex marriage, the marriage would be regarded as valid in the party's country of domicile.
- If you are in a qualifying civil partnership you can change it to a marriage – a qualifying civil partnership is a civil partnership which was registered in Scotland, England, Wales or Northern Ireland and has not been dissolved,

annulled or ended by death or an overseas relationship registered out with the United Kingdom which is treated as a civil partnership in Scotland and has not been dissolved, annulled or ended by death.

Types of marriage

You can be married in either of two ways in Scotland - by a religious or belief ceremony or by a civil ceremony:

- A religious or belief marriage may take place anywhere and may be solemnised only by a minister, clergyman, pastor, priest or other person approved to do so under the Marriage (Scotland) Act 1977.
- A civil marriage may take place in a registration office or at any place agreed between the registration authority and the couple and may be solemnised only by a registrar or an assistant registrar who has been authorised by the Registrar General for that purpose.

How and when to give notice

You can each obtain a marriage notice form, and information about fees, from any registrar of births etc. in Scotland. In most cases you can get the address of your local registrar from the telephone directory. A list of registrars is also available on the NRS website at www.nrscotland.gov.uk/files/registration/reglist.pdf.

Each of you must complete and submit a marriage notice, along with the required documents (see below) and the appropriate fee, to the registrar for the district in which the marriage is to take place. This means that both parties must be aware of the marriage and independently complete and sign the declaration on the marriage notice form. Failing to give proper notice can result in a marriage being postponed or prevented from proceeding.

Timing is important. The notices must be submitted early enough to enable the registrar to satisfy themself that you are free to marry one another. Normally notices should be in their hands about TEN to TWELVE weeks beforehand. The minimum period is 29 days before the date of the proposed marriage, but if you leave things as late as this you could be faced with the need to postpone your marriage.

Only in exceptional circumstances will the Registrar General authorise a marriage to take place if 29 days' notice has not been given.

Although you need not both attend personally at the registrar's office to hand in your marriage notice, at least one of you may be asked to attend there personally before the date of the marriage. This is necessary, in the case of a religious or belief marriage, to collect the Marriage Schedule (see page 4) or, it might be necessary in the case of a civil marriage, to finalise arrangements with the registrar.

Every person giving notice is required to sign a declaration to the effect that the particulars and information given on the notice are correct. As a safeguard against bigamous marriages a subsequent check of the information is made by NRS.

If you live in England or Wales

As an alternative to the normal procedure of giving notice to a registrar in Scotland, if you intend to marry

(i) a person residing in Scotland, or (ii) a person residing in England or Wales who has a parent residing in Scotland, you may give notice of marriage to the superintendent registrar in the district of England or Wales in which you reside. The person you are marrying should, however, give notice in Scotland in the usual way.

You should seek the advice of the superintendent registrar if you wish to proceed in this way. The certificate for marriage obtained from him should be sent to the Scottish registrar as quickly as possible.

Documents to be produced

When giving or sending the marriage notice forms to the registrar each of you must supply the following:

- Your birth certificate or, if you are adopted, your adoption certificate.
- Evidence of your usual residence.
- If you have been married or in a registered civil partnership before and the marriage or civil partnership has been

116

dissolved or annulled, a decree of divorce or dissolution or annulment or a certified copy decree. A decree of divorce or dissolution granted out with Scotland must be absolute or final - a decree nisi is not acceptable.

- The registrar will ask to see your valid passport or other document to provide evidence of your nationality.

- If your spouse or civil partner is deceased, the death certificate of your former spouse or civil partner.

- If you are in a qualifying civil partnership, an extract from the entry in the civil partnership register relating to the civil partnership.

- If you are in an existing marriage, your marriage certificate.

- If your domicile is abroad, a certificate of no impediment issued by the competent authority to the effect that you are free to marry.

- If any of these documents are in a language other than English, a certified translation in English must also be provided.

- Do not delay giving notice simply because you are waiting for any of the documents mentioned above to come to hand. If time is getting short it is better to give notice first and then pass the documents to the registrar when they become available; but they must be made available to the registrar before the marriage. Provided the documents are in order, the marriage can proceed as arranged.

If you are subject to immigration controls you will have to provide extra documentation to that outlined above. In particular, you will need to provide a Declaration of Immigration Status form which can be obtained from the registrar or the NRS website. Evidence to support the statement you make on the Declaration of Immigration Status form will also be required. If you are in any doubt about what is required, or if you need further information, you should consult the registrar or contact NRS.

If you are domiciled outside the United Kingdom

The normal procedure of giving notice to the registrar in Scotland must be followed but, as previously mentioned, an additional requirement is placed upon you.

If, being domiciled in a country outside the UK, you are subject to the marriage laws of that country, you should obtain, if practicable, a certificate issued by the competent authority (usually the civil authority) in that country to the effect that there is no impediment to your proposed marriage. If the certificate is in a language other than English you should also produce a certified translation.

In the absence of such a certificate without good reason being shown, it may not be possible for you to marry in Scotland.

If you are now resident in the UK, and have lived here for the last two years or more, you need not submit such a certificate.

If you are a UK citizen living abroad, or an Australian or New Zealand or Canadian or United States of America citizen you need not submit such a certificate.

Making arrangements for the marriage ceremony

It is important to make early arrangements for the date and time of your marriage.

- If you are having a religious or belief ceremony, contact the person performing the marriage before completing the notice of marriage.

- For a civil marriage, make advance arrangements with the registrar. This is particularly important if the ceremony is to be in towns and cities, where large numbers of people want to be married at certain times of the year.

- Arrange for two persons, aged 16 years or over, to be present at your marriage to act as witnesses. They are required whether it is a religious or belief or civil ceremony.

- Be sure to let the person performing the marriage know if you change your plans or decide to postpone your marriage.

THE MARRIAGE SCHEDULE

When they are satisfied there is no legal impediment to the marriage, the registrar will prepare a Marriage Schedule from the information you have given them. The Schedule is a most important document - no marriage can proceed without it.

If you are having a religious or belief marriage the Marriage Schedule will be issued to you by the registrar. The Schedule cannot be issued more than seven days before the marriage and the registrar will advise you when to call to collect it. The Schedule cannot be collected on your behalf by a relative or friend - the registrar will issue it only to one of the parties to the marriage.

- The Marriage Schedule must be produced before the marriage ceremony to the person performing the marriage.

- Immediately after the ceremony, the Schedule must be signed in black fountain pen by both parties, by the person performing the marriage and by the two witnesses. Thereafter, it must be returned to the registrar within three days so that (s)he can register the marriage.

- If you are having a civil marriage, a Marriage Schedule will not be issued, but the registrar will have it available at the marriage ceremony for signature. Subsequently, the registrar will register the marriage.

- A fee for the civil marriage and, if applicable, for the attendance of an authorised registrar if the location is somewhere other than the registration office, is payable to the registrar in advance.

The marriage certificate

After the marriage has been registered, you can obtain copies of the marriage certificate from the registrar on payment of the appropriate fee.

Degrees of relationship within which marriage is unlawful

1. Relationships by consanguinity

Parent Child Grandparent Grandchild Sibling Aunt or uncle Niece or nephew Great-grandparent Great-grandchild

2. Relationships by affinity

Child of former spouse Child of former civil partner Former spouse of parent Former civil partner of parent Former spouse of grandparent Former civil partner of grandparent Grandchild of former spouse Grandchild of former civil partner

3. Relationships by adoption

Adoptive parent or former adoptive parent Adopted child or former adopted child

Divorce and dissolution

Ending a marriage

When your marriage comes to an end, you will probably have a number of things to sort out with your partner, which may include childcare, money, housing, and other property and possessions.

You and/or your partner could decide:-

- to separate informally, without going to court
- to separate by drawing up a separation agreement
- to end your marriage formally by getting a divorce
- to get a decree of nullity

If you're not a British Citizen

If you're not a British Citizen and your marriage ends, this could affect your right to stay in the UK. If you're not a British Citizen and you are thinking of ending your marriage, you should get advice from an experienced immigration adviser. Your local Citizens Advice Bureau should be able to help - where to get advice.

Separating informally

If you and your partner are married, you can separate by an informal arrangement. You will need to inform:

- your benefits office if you are getting a welfare benefit such as Jobseeker's Allowance, Income-related Employment and Support Allowance or Income Support
- HM Revenue and Customs if you are getting tax credits
- your local council if you pay council tax or you get Housing Benefit or Council Tax Reduction.

If you and your partner agree, you can make arrangements about children, money, housing and other property without going to court. However, any informal arrangement made when you separate may affect future decisions if you do go to court. If there are children the Child Maintenance Service may get involved. If you do decide later to divorce and the court is involved it can change an arrangement made informally by a couple that it considers to be unreasonable or, in the case of a child, if it thinks the arrangement is not in the child's best interests.

Separating with a separation agreement

A separation agreement is a written agreement between a couple who intend to stop living together. It sets out how they wish to sort out financial arrangements, property and arrangements for the children. When your agreement includes financial matters it should be made with the help of a solicitor. Examples of what you might want to include in an agreement are:-

- to live separately. This stops both partners from having to live together
- not to molest, annoy or disturb the other partner
- to provide financial support (maintenance) for the other partner. A separation agreement would normally say that maintenance will stop if the partner starts living together with a different partner. Any agreement not to apply to court in the future for financial support does not count legally
- to provide financial support (maintenance) for any children of the relationship. Any agreement not to apply to a court or to the Child Maintenance Service in the future is not valid legally
- who the children should live and have contact with.

The advantage of a written agreement is that it is easier to make sure you both understand what has been agreed. It also means that either partner can go to court to change the agreement in the future. The court may only change what it considers to be unfair or unreasonable. It is advisable to consult a solicitor when drawing up a separation agreement, but you should work out in advance the general areas you want to cover as listed above - where to get advice.

If you can reduce the time it takes to draw up the agreement with the solicitor it could keep legal costs down. You may get help with your legal costs.

Judicial separation

A judicial separation is a court order which stops the obligation of the partners of a marriage having to live together. It is quite rare to get a judicial separation, but it can be used by couples who have a moral or religious objection to divorce. The order does not end the marriage so neither partner is free to marry again (or enter into a civil partnership). The order does not change each partner's rights to stay in the family home. If you want your partner to leave, after a judicial separation, and s/he is not willing to, you have to go to court for an exclusion order.

Decree of nullity

For a marriage to be legal, it must meet certain conditions. For example, you and your partner must both be over 16 when you marry and you must not already be a civil partner or married to someone else. If your marriage does not meet one of these conditions, the court can end the marriage by granting an annulment.

When the court grants an annulment, it may say that your marriage is:-

void. This means that, in effect, the marriage never existed; or

voidable. This means the marriage was legal at the time it was registered but it isn't legal any longer. Whether the court will say your marriage is void or voidable depends on the circumstances.

If you have children, the court will not grant an annulment unless it is satisfied about the arrangements for the children.
You will need to get legal advice if you want to apply for an annulment. You might get financial help to pay for your legal costs.

You can only get a divorce in Scotland if you satisfy certain rules about where you both live. The rules are complicated and you should get more advice from a Citizens Advice Bureau. In order to get divorced the marriage must be recognised as valid in the United Kingdom. There are two ways to get a divorce:-

- the simplified procedure, often called DIY divorce; or
- the ordinary procedure.
- DIY divorce

If you have no children under 16 and can agree about how to deal with your money and property you can use a simplified procedure to get a divorce. You don't have to use a solicitor so you can keep the costs of the divorce low.

You can use forms to apply for a DIY divorce from your local sheriff court or the Scottish Courts and Tribunals Service website at www.scotcourts.gov.uk. There is also some useful guidance on DIY divorce proceedings on the Scottish Courts and Tribunals Service website at www.scotcourts.gov.uk. You may find it helpful to get more advice before you apply. You can get more comprehensive advice from your local CAB.

Ordinary divorce procedure

If you have children under 16 you have to use the ordinary procedure to get a divorce. If you can agree about the grounds for divorce and what to do about the children, money and property the divorce can go to court as an undefended case.

If you cannot agree about the grounds for the divorce, or issues about the children, money or property the divorce application will go to court as a defended case.

Undefended divorce

In an undefended divorce, it will be advisable to go to a solicitor for general advice before you apply for a divorce. A solicitor can be useful for advice on whether there are sufficient grounds, which grounds are appropriate and what evidence may be needed. The solicitor will help you to draw up an agreement that can be lodged in court. If there are disputes about children, property or money which you and your partner can't resolve, you will have to consult a solicitor or mediator to resolve the problems before the case can go to court as an undefended case.

Defended divorce

A defended divorce will normally be heard in the sheriff court, although the case can be transferred to the Court of Session if the issues that have to be resolved are complicated or there is a lot of money or property to make decisions about.

In a defended divorce, both partners should always consult a solicitor. Legal fees can be very high if there are long disputes. It is advisable wherever possible for you both to try to come to an agreement about as much as possible before going to court.

What do you have to prove to get a divorce

There are two grounds for divorce:-

- the marriage has broken down irretrievably
- one of the partners to the marriage has an interim gender recognition certificate.

If you are getting divorced on the grounds that your marriage has broken down irretrievably you or your partner will have to show that the marriage no longer exists on a permanent basis. Legally, this is called an irretrievable breakdown of the marriage. The irretrievable breakdown of the marriage can be proved in one of the following ways:-

- your partner has behaved unreasonably
- adultery
- you've lived apart for at least one year and you both agree to the divorce
- you've lived apart for at least two years but one of you doesn't agree to the divorce.

Adultery

A court may grant a divorce if one of you has had a sexual relationship with someone else of the opposite sex (committed adultery). If you or your partner has had a sexual relationship with someone else of the same sex it is not technically adultery but is likely to be seen as evidence of irretrievable breakdown.

The court will need details of the adultery, for example, dates and places when it happened. The court will only grant the divorce if it is satisfied that the marriage has irretrievably broken down and the other partner could no longer live with the partner who has committed adultery. There is no minimum period that you have to be married before a divorce action based on adultery may be started.

If you both agree to the divorce, the court will usually only need statements and details of the adulterous sexual relationship. If one of you doesn't agree to the divorce, proof will be necessary and this may be difficult and expensive to get.

Unreasonable behaviour

A court may grant a divorce if you or your partner has behaved so badly that the other can no longer bear living together. Unreasonable behaviour can include mental or physical cruelty, including violence or abuse, and less obvious things like dominating a partner, not letting the partner leave the home or speak to neighbours and friends or refusing to pay for housekeeping.

If one of you doesn't agree to the divorce, evidence and details will be needed, for example, evidence from witnesses such as friends or medical evidence.

If your partner has been violent towards you, you should get specialist help.

Living apart for one year

If you have lived apart (been separated) for one year and you both agree to a divorce, a court will accept this as proof of irretrievable breakdown of the marriage. The one year of living apart will still be considered as continuous even if you have actually got back together for up to six months within that time. The six month period of being back together cannot be used to count towards the one year of living apart. For example if a couple separates in January, gets back together in April but splits again in September the first three months of separation still count towards the year apart. Separation may be used as a ground for divorce even when you and your spouse have lived in the same home but only if you are no longer living as a married couple and effectively lead separate lives.

Living apart for two years

If you have lived apart (been separated) for two years continuously, you can apply for a divorce without your partner's agreement. A court will usually agree to a divorce if you have been separated for two years. Separation may be used as a ground for divorce even when you and your spouse have lived in the same home but only if you are no longer living as a married couple and effectively lead separate lives.

Applying for an interim gender recognition certificate

A transsexual person who has an interim gender recognition certificate can end her/his marriage on this ground. S/he must apply to a Gender Recognition Panel.

129

For more information see www.gov.uk.

Applying for a divorce

The partner who is applying for the divorce is called the pursuer. The other partner is the defender. If you want to start divorce proceedings you will need to get the forms from the sheriff court or the Scottish Courts and Tribunals Service website at www.scotcourts.gov.uk for a DIY divorce. You have to use a solicitor to start a divorce action under the ordinary procedure. If you are applying for a divorce and want help to fill in the forms, you should consult an experienced adviser, for example, at a Citizens Advice Bureau - where to get advice.

What the court will do-If you both agree to the divorce

If you both agree to the divorce, the court will look at the paperwork that has been submitted. Under the ordinary procedure it will be submitted by the solicitor and is likely to include a summons (or initial writ) and the sworn statements (affidavits) made by the pursuer and any witnesses.

If you have children, the court will need to be satisfied that you have made satisfactory arrangements for them. The court may want to discuss the arrangements and possibly meet the children if they are old enough. A divorce which you both agree to can take up to six months if there are no children or money issues involved. It can take longer if children are involved and the court is not satisfied with the arrangements being made for them. For more information about arrangements for the children, see under heading Children at the end of a marriage. When the court agrees to grant the divorce it issues a divorce certificate called an extract decree of divorce.

If one of you doesn't agree to the divorce

If you start divorce proceedings and your partner doesn't agree about the grounds for divorce or arrangements for children or property s/he will have to send a Notice of Intention to defend to the court when s/he first receives the initial writ from the court. S/he has to say why s/he doesn't agree that the marriage has broken down. There is likely to be a court hearing for a judge to decide whether the marriage has broken down irretrievably.

Even if the court agrees that the marriage has broken down, it has to be satisfied that you have made satisfactory arrangements for any children. They may want to discuss arrangements about the children and possibly meet them if they are old enough. For more information about arrangements for the children, see under heading Children at the end of a marriage.

If the court agrees to grant the divorce, they will issue a divorce certificate called an extract decree of divorce.

Help with the legal costs of a divorce

You may be able to get help with legal costs. Whether or not you get it depends on both you and your partner's income, capital and how reasonable the Scottish Legal Aid Board thinks it is to give you help. If you do get help, in some cases you might have to pay some of the legal costs back, out of money or property you are given when the divorce comes through. This is called clawback. Make sure your solicitor explains clawback to you before you start the case.

Children at the end of a marriage

When you stop living together, you'll have to decide who will look after the children.

You may be able to make arrangements between yourselves about where the children are to live and what contact should take place with the other parent. However, if this is not possible, the court can make the decisions about the children.

The Scottish Government has produced a parenting pack that explores all the issues. It is available at www.gov.scot.

Many couples split up but never get divorced. If you separate informally, you may not ever need to go to court. You can make arrangements for the children that may last until the children are grown up. But if it is not possible to sort out the arrangements, the court can make decisions.

If you are getting a divorce, the court will not grant the divorce until it has looked at the arrangements for the children. The court is primarily concerned about the children's welfare. You'll have to give the names of all dependent children of the family. Children under 16 are usually thought of as dependent. The duty to provide for (maintain) a child usually lasts until a child is 18 or 19 if in full-time non-advanced education or if in full time further education up to 25. The court will want details of children who are the children of both partners together, adopted children, step-children and any children who have been treated as part of the family. It doesn't include foster children.

You have to give details of how the children will be looked after. You'll need to say where the children will live and who they will live with, as well as the financial arrangements for their support. The court's main concern will be to decide what's in the best interests of the children. If the court is satisfied that the arrangements made by the parents for the children are in their best interests it will not change them. It will only make decisions where this is necessary to sort out a disagreement about arrangements. Decisions made by the court are called orders. You could get help from a mediator or collaborative law practitioner to make arrangements about the children, see under heading Family mediation or collaboration.

If you are thinking of going to court about arrangements for your children, you should consult an experienced adviser, for example, a family law solicitor or go to a Citizens Advice

What orders can a court make about children

A court will only make an order concerning children if it feels it is in the best interests of the children to do so.

A court can make orders about:-

- who the child should live with (a residence order)
- who the child should have contact with and what sort of contact it should be (a contact order)
- preventing something happening, for example, a name change

- specific issues.
- Residence orders

The court can make a residence order in favour of:-

- one parent. This means that the child must live with that parent
- both parents. One residence order can be made for both parents, even if they are not living together. The order will say how much time the child will live with each parent
- a third person, for example, a grandparent.

Contact orders

The court will normally expect you and your partner to make your own arrangements about maintaining contact with your children. The court will only make a court order if you can't agree.

The contact order may include conditions. It may also say what sort of contact you can have, for example, visiting, telephoning or writing letters. Orders can also be made to allow contact between a child and other relatives or friends.

Preventing something from happening

A court can make an order called an interdict to prevent one parent from doing something that the court thinks is not in the child's best interests.

Specific issues

A court can make an order about a specific issue that a child's parents cannot agree about, for example, religious education.

Household goods and other possessions

If a couple split up and they disagree about who owns household goods and possessions acquired during the marriage it is presumed they are owned jointly. Gifts and inherited goods belong to the person who received them. Goods acquired before the marriage belong to the person who acquired them. If you cannot agree about who owns all the goods and possessions you may need help. It may be useful to ask a mediator or collaborative law practitioner for help as going to court is expensive. If you are having to go to court about other financial matters any disputes about valuable goods may have to be dealt with at the same time. You should ask your solicitor about disputes about household goods and possessions.

Financial arrangements at the end of a marriage

Until you are divorced you and your spouse have a legal obligation to provide financial support for each other.

.

For the spouses-Agreeing financial support for each spouse

If you both agree to financial support, this is called a voluntary agreement. It can be written down or it could be a verbal agreement. You can agree, for example, that one of you will make weekly payments to the other for the support of children, or will meet rent or mortgage payments and household bills or pay for the children's clothing and holidays.

Before you agree on a package of financial support, you should get legal advice about whether it is an appropriate arrangement. It may be useful to have an agreement written up by a solicitor in case of future dispute. You might get help with the costs of making a voluntary agreement.

Court orders for money from a former spouse

You can apply for a court order for financial support at the end of a marriage. The court will consider all financial circumstances of both partners, including pension arrangements. A court can make an order for regular payments to be made or for a one-off lump sum. It can also make an order about pension arrangements.

You might get help with legal costs when you apply to court for financial support. However, you might have to pay some of the legal costs back, out of money or property you are given by the court order. This is called clawback. Make sure your solicitor explains clawback properly to you before you start court action. Where pension arrangements are involved, you should also consider getting specialist financial advice.

For children
Agreeing financial support for children

If you both agree to financial support, this is called a voluntary agreement or family-based arrangement. It can be written down or it could be a verbal agreement. You can agree, for example, that one of you will make weekly payments to the other for the support of children, or will meet rent or mortgage payments and household bills, or pay for the children's clothing and holidays.

If you need advice on the options available for arranging child maintenance and for advice on how to set up a voluntary child maintenance agreement, you can contact the Child Maintenance Options Service at www.cmoptions.org.

The Child Maintenance Options Service can help you:-
- understand the options for making a child maintenance agreement
- check that any existing arrangement is right for you and your child
- estimate how much child maintenance you would pay or get
- refer you to other organisations for help and advice.

Before you agree on a package of financial support, it may be useful to get legal advice about whether it is an appropriate arrangement. It may be useful to have an agreement written up by a solicitor in case of future dispute. You might get help with the costs of making a voluntary agreement.

.

Child Maintenance Service (CMS)
If your marriage has ended and the children are living with you, you can use the Child Maintenance Service (CMS) to get financial support for your children. However you don't have to use the CMS if you don't want to. The CMS is the government child maintenance

service that arranges maintenance for children under the 2012 scheme.

Housing rights at the end of a marriage

At the end of your marriage, the court can give you or your partner rights to the home or can take rights to occupy the home away from either of you. As long as you are both still living in the home, whether it is owned or rented, you both have rights to live in it. If one partner has been violent there are special orders the court can make to change the violent partner's rights to the home and exclude her/him.

If one of you is a sole owner or a sole tenant and the other partner leaves the home, s/he may have to go to court to enforce her/his rights to get back in. If you are thinking of going to court about your housing rights after the breakdown of your marriage, you should consult an experienced adviser, for example, a family law solicitor or a Citizens Advice.

If you and your partner are owner-occupiers the value of the family home is likely to be an issue within the divorce settlement. You should see an experienced adviser about decisions that can be made about the family home.

Housing costs at the end of a marriage
Paying the mortgage when a marriage breaks down

If a mortgage is in joint names, both people are jointly and solely liable for the mortgage payments. This is known as joint and several liability. This means that if one of you leaves and stops contributing

138

to the mortgage payments, the mortgage lender can ask the other person to pay the full amount.

If a mortgage is in one person's name, only that person is liable for the mortgage payments. However, if your name is not on the mortgage and you want to stay in your home, you will need to keep up the mortgage payments. If your ex-partner is no longer making any payments, you will need to pay the full amount, otherwise the mortgage lender can start action to repossess your home. Get in touch with the lender and negotiate what payments might be accepted to stay in the home. You have the right to do this because you are married.

Paying the rent when a marriage breaks down
Joint tenancy

A joint tenancy means that all of the tenants named on the tenancy agreement are jointly and solely liable for the rent. This is known as joint and several liability. This means that if the other joint tenant leaves and stops making payments towards the rent, the landlord can ask you to pay the full amount. That's why it's important to keep paying the full amount, otherwise you may get evicted. In some cases, a joint tenant can end the joint tenancy by giving notice to the landlord. If you want to stay in the property you'll need to make sure this doesn't happen or if it has happened, you can negotiate with the landlord. Your landlord may be able to give you a new tenancy in your name only. If you are in this situation you should get advice.

Sole tenancy which is not in your name

If a tenancy is in the name of your married partner, they will be liable to pay the rent for as long as the tenancy continues. If the rent isn't paid and arrears build up, the landlord may take action to evict you. If your ex-partner is no longer paying any rent, you should negotiate with the landlord to pay the rent because you have the right to do so. If the landlord won't accept the rent you should get advice straightaway. If there are arrears you should also get advice about how to pay these off if you want to stay in the home.

Benefits and housing costs

If you stay in your home after your partner has left, depending on your income, you may be able to get Housing Benefit to help pay the rent. If there is a mortgage, you might get help with the mortgage interest.

Family mediation or collaboration

Family mediation and collaborative practice are two ways of helping couples who are separating or divorcing to sort out disagreements and reach decisions about things like money, property and looking after the children, without having to go to court. To use either of these options, you both have to be willing to go along voluntarily. Any decisions you make there will not be legally binding but may help you to start drawing up an agreement. Mediation involves you working together with your partner and a trained, impartial mediator, to reach agreement. Collaborative practice involves you and your partner meeting together with your solicitors, to discuss the issues and try to reach agreement.

A couple can use family mediation or collaborative practice as soon as possible after they have decided their relationship is ending and they feel able to discuss any disputes. Mediation and collaborative practice can be helpful before legal proceedings begin, to encourage co-operation between the couple and to prevent disputes from getting worse and agreement becoming harder to reach in the future. They can also be used after a separation or divorce if new issues arise or there are outstanding issues to be resolved.

There may be an additional need for children to be able to say how they feel. There is a specialist service called family decision-making that aims to reduce conflict and distress to make better decisions as a family.

For more information about mediation and a national map of local services, see www.relationships-scotland.org.uk.

Some local solicitors may be skilled in family mediation. You can check what is available in your area by contacting The Law Society of Scotland:

The Law Society of Scotland
Atria One
144 Morrison Street
Edinburgh
EH3 8EX
Tel: 0131 226 7411

Fax: 0131 225 2934

E-mail: lawscot@lawscot.org.uk

Website: www.lawscot.org.uk

The Spark

The Spark provides relationship counselling services for families, couples, individuals and young people and has regional centres across Scotland where clients can access face to face counselling. Telephone and online counselling is also available. There is a charge for counselling but what you have to pay can be negotiated. The Spark has a relationship helpline offering immediate relationship support. Calls are free from landlines and mobile networks. If you prefer to type rather than talk you can use the webchat instant messaging support service which you can access from the top of the homepage of the website. The contact details are:-

The Spark

General enquiries: 0808 802 0050

Relationship Helpline: 0808 802 2088 (Mon, Wed and Thurs 11am-2pm).

Appointments: 0808 802 0050

Email: Contact form available on the website

Website: www.thespark.org.uk

Family Decision Making Service

If there are problems in the family because of divorce, separation of parents or other carers there are agencies that can help you all to make sure everyone knows how children feel before any decisions are taken. The Family Decision Making Service is run by three organisations all together - One Parent Families Scotland, Parentline Scotland and the Scottish Child Law Centre. They aim to help to reduce conflict and improve collaboration between separated and separating parents using family group decision-making. You can read more about this service on the website of One Parent Families Scotland.

Same sex marriages-Divorce

If a same sex marriage breaks down, the couple can move for a divorce. You can only get a same sex divorce by applying to the court, usually the Sheriff Court, to grant a decree of divorce. If you and your spouse can agree on any issues arising from the separation before applying for divorce, the application for divorce is then undefended. This means that neither party has to go to court to give evidence for the divorce, and makes the whole process much more straightforward. You will usually need a solicitor to draft and submit the application for you.

If, however, you cannot agree, you may have to raise a court action for the court to resolve the issues as part of the divorce proceedings. This can be a costly process with solicitor representation on both sides.

A same sex divorce can be applied for under two different procedures, depending on your circumstances:

- Simplified/ 'DIY' procedure – this is also referred to as a 'quickie divorce' or 'DIY divorce', and may apply to you if there are no financial matters to resolve, or these have already been decided and drawn up in a formal Separation Agreement, and there are no children under 16 of the marriage.

• Ordinary procedure – in all other cases.

In order to apply for a divorce, you first need to establish grounds for divorce.

Grounds for divorce

There are only two grounds you can use for same sex divorce. The most common ground is if you can establish that the marriage has broken down irretrievably. There are three different ways you can show irretrievable breakdown of the marriage:

1. You have been separated from your spouse for one year and your spouse is prepared to consent to the dissolution.

2. You have been separated from your spouse for two years. You can then go ahead with a dissolution without your spouse's consent.

3. You can establish that your spouse's behaviour is such that you cannot reasonably be expected to continue to live with them – this is often referred to as 'unreasonable behaviour'. You can then apply for a divorce immediately. You would have to provide evidence from someone else to confirm the position. Unreasonable behaviour does not necessarily mean just physical abuse. It can also cover issues such as alcohol or drug abuse or gambling, as well as emotional abuse.

These grounds are largely the same as for heterosexual couples on divorce with the exception of adultery, which is not currently a ground for same sex divorce. This is due to its definition (adultery is defined in the common law as voluntary sexual intercourse between a spouse and a person of the opposite sex outside of the marriage). However, adultery would be a ground if a spouse in a same sex marriage was unfaithful with a member of the opposite sex. For a spouse in a same sex marriage who has discovered that their partner has been unfaithful with a member of the same sex, they could consider applying for divorce on the ground of their partner's behaviour instead.

The second ground for divorce is where an interim gender recognition certificate has been granted. Previously, the Gender Recognition Act 2004 required a person undergoing gender recognition treatment to be divorced (or their civil partnership dissolved), before they would be given their full Gender Recognition Certificate. That was on the basis that same sex marriage was not legal. Now, couples can change gender without the need to seek a divorce or dissolution of their Civil Partnership.

Same sex spouses are entitled to the same financial provision as heterosexual spouses on divorce

Length of time to obtain divorce
This will depend upon your circumstances and what childcare and financial arrangements need to be sorted out. However, if those have already been resolved, or if there are no such matters to sort out, then an uncontested divorce can be granted within six to eight

145

weeks, assuming there are no other complications (such as locating your spouse or serving papers on them).

Ending a civil partnership

A civil partnership can be ended in the same way as a marriage, that is, by applying to the sheriff court for a dissolution. This works in the same way as divorce. A dissolution will only be granted if the civil partnership has irretrievably broken down (or if an interim gender recognition certificate has been issued to either partner. Irretrievable breakdown can be established by proving one of these circumstances

- 'unreasonable behaviour' – the partner applying for the dissolution shows that the other partner has behaved in such a way that it would be unreasonable to expect the applicant partner to continue living with them. This behaviour could include domestic abuse for example, and depending on the circumstances could also include sexual infidelity.
- the partners have lived apart for one year and they both agree to the dissolution.
- the partners have lived apart for two years and only one of them wants the dissolution.

These are the same rules as for divorce. For divorce, irretrievable breakdown of marriage can also be proved by proving adultery, defined as heterosexual sexual intercourse with someone other than the spouse. For civil partnership dissolution, sexual infidelity would be included under the unreasonable behaviour ground for dissolution, as is the case for any sexual infidelity in marriage that is not heterosexual intercourse.

When the court grants a dissolution of civil partnership, it can rule on a division of property between the partners. The rules are the same as for property division on divorce: the basic rule is that any property obtained by either partner during the partnership (except gifts or bequests to made to one or the other partner) is split equally between the partners. The court can also rule on residence and contact arrangements for any children who the couple have been parenting.

Parenting

The rules on parenting have in the past been significantly different for married couples and for civil partners. The differences have been removed by the Adoption and Children (Scotland) Act 2007 and the Human Fertilisation and Embryology Act 2008.

****

USEFUL INFORMATION

This book is designed to give you as much information as possible and to prepare you for the legalities of the divorce procedure. There are many other sources of information about divorce and the various aspects of divorce such as welfare benefits etc. The following are some of the more useful addresses and web sites.

Alcoholics Anonymous

National Helpline 0800 9177 650

Web site: www.alcoholics-anonymous.org.uk

Asian Family Counselling Service

Suite 51

Windmill Place

2-4 Windmill Lane

Southhall

Middlesex

UB2 4NJ

Tel: 0208 571 3933

Association for Shared Parenting

0300 121 0131

Web site:

www.sharedparenting.org.uk

Child Abduction Unit

www.gov.uk/return-or-contact-abducted-child

Child Poverty Action Group

30 Micawber Street

London

N1 7TB

Tel: 020 7837 7979

Fax: 020 7253 0599

Web site: www.cpag.org.uk

Child Maintenance Options

Enquiry line tel: 0800 988 0988

www.cmoptions.org.

Family Law Consortium

1 Henrietta Street

London

WC2 8PS

www.lawyer-solicitors-uk.co.uk

Forced Marriage Unit

www.gov.uk/guidance/forced-marriage

Gingerbread

Single Parent Helpline 0207 428 5400

Web site: www.gingerbread.org.uk.

A support organisation for lone parents and their families, with around 20 centres in the country.

Women's Aid

Women's Aid Federation of England,
PO BOX 3245
Bristol,
BS2 2EH, England
National helpline: Tel: 0808 2000247
www.womensaid.org.uk

National Council for the Divorced and Separated

45 Russell Road, London E4 8HA
Phone: 070 4147 8120
ncdsw.org.uk

National Family Mediation

National Family Mediation,
1st Floor, Civic Centre,
Paris St, Exeter
EX1 1JN
Phone: 0300 4000 636
www.nfm.org.uk

Relate National Marriage Guidance Council

National Phoneline 0300 100 1234

Website: www.relate.org.uk

Scottish Marriage Care
72 Waterloo Street
Glasgow
G2 7DA
Relationship Helpline 0808 802 2088
www.thespark.org.uk

Scottish Legal Aid Board
The Scottish Legal Aid Board
Thistle House
91 Haymarket Terrace
Edinburgh
EH12 5HE
0131 226 7061

Scottish Women's Aid
132 Rose Street
Edinburgh EH2 3JD
0800 027 1234

Further information-civil partnerships
Stonewall can provide information on www.stonewall.org.uk

Northern Ireland information on civil partnerships www.nidirect.gov.uk/articles/guidance-civil-partnerships.

Tax-contact your local tax office or go to www.hmrc.gov.uk

Pensions-contact the pension service on www.gov.uk/contact-pension-service

Tax credits contact www.gov.uk/browse/benefits/tax-credits

Child Benefit- contact the child Benefit Help line on 0845 609 0082 e-mail child.benefit@hmrc.gsi.gov.uk

Child Maintenance Options 0800 0835 130

****

LIST OF THE MAIN COUNTY COURT FORMS (ENGLAND AND WALES) AND APPLICATIONS USED IN DIVORCE/DISSOLUTION PROCEEDINGS. THE MAIN FORMS FOR BOTH DIVORCE AND DISSOLUTION HAVE BEEN AMALGAMATED.

Leaflets to read before commencing divorce:/dissolution

D183 ABOUT DIVORCE/DISSOLUTION

D184 I WANT A DIVORCE/DISSOLUTION-WHAT DO I DO?

D185 CHILDREN AND DIVORCE

D186 THE RESPONDENT HAS REPLIED TO MY PETITION-WHAT DO I DO?

D187 I HAVE A DECREE NISI-WHAT DO I DO NEXT?

D190-I WANT TO APPLY FOR A FINANCIAL ORDER

The forms (which can be obtained from www.hmcourtservice.org

1. PETITION FOR DIVORCE/Dissolution of Civil Partnership (form D8)
2. Notes for guidance (Petition)
3. Statement of Arrangements for Children (form D8A)
4. Notice of Application (form D11)
5. Affidavit in support of an application to dispense with service of the petition on the respondent (form D13b)
6. Notice of Application for Decree Nisi to be made Absolute (form D36)
7. Affidavit of means (form D75)

Index

****